Guide to Part G
of the Building Regulations
Sanitation, hot water safety and water efficiency

2010 Edition

Nick Price

© RIBA Enterprises, 2010

Published by NBS, 15 Bonhill Street, London EC2P 2EA

ISBN 978 1 85946 333 8

Stock code 69153

British Library Cataloguing in Publications Data
A catalogue record for this book is available from the British Library.

Publisher: Steven Cross
Commissioning Editor: Lucy Harbor
Project Editor: Prepress Projects Ltd, Perth, UK
Designed by Phillip Handley
Typeset by Prepress Projects Ltd, Perth, UK
Printed and bound by Thanet Press, Kent

While every effort has been made to check the accuracy and quality of the information given in this publication, neither the Author nor the Publisher accept any responsibility for the subsequent use of this information, for any errors or omissions that it may contain, or for any misunderstandings arising from it.

NBS is part of RIBA Enterprises Ltd.
www.ribaenterprises.com

Contents

Foreword

The Approved Document to Part G of the Building Regulations was first published in 1985 with the title 'Hygiene' and contained four elements: food storage, bathrooms, hot water storage and sanitary conveniences.

When it was published again in 1990, food storage was removed. In 2000 Part G was revised along with the Building Regulations 2000 (which replaced the Building Regulations 1991), and when it was subsequently amended in 2002 it contained the same three elements as previously but renumbered.

Since then there have been many changes to the way that water and sanitation are used in the UK and amendments to the numerous supporting documents and Standards, but until now Part G remained unchanged. In April 2010 a new Approved Document to Part G was published with the new title of 'Sanitation, hot water safety and water efficiency'.

This document is a radical departure from the previous Part G series of Approved Documents, and it now contains six elements: cold water supply; water efficiency; hot water supply and systems; sanitary conveniences and washing facilities; bathrooms; and kitchens and food preparation areas.

Approved Documents are often considered to be de facto Regulations, but they are in fact mainly guidance to the actual Regulations. The short statements in green at the beginning of each section are the legal requirements, but the remainder of the document purely provides suggestions as to how to meet the requirements. This is useful in that, when unusual situations arise, alternative solutions can be considered, but it can lead to uncertainty and different interpretations of how to achieve the requirements. This is why books such as this guide are needed.

Furthermore, many of the documents that are called up by the Approved Documents are rather voluminous and expensive. This guide contains the relevant extracts from the key documents so that this can be a one-stop-shop for all the issues related to Part G of the Building Regulations. As so much of Part G is concerned with plumbing and heating engineering, the Chartered Institute of Plumbing and Heating Engineering (CIPHE) is pleased to be able to contribute this foreword to the Guide.

John Griggs
Principal Technical Officer
CIPHE
May 2010

General introduction

0.1   Introduction to the guide

Designers are faced with constant change: in regulation, standards, technology, materials and methods. This is exacerbated not by lack of information, but by its abundance, particularly as web searches often give tens of pages of references, which may or may not be relevant or up to date. This guide is intended to act as an immediate source of advice to make compliance with the requirements of Part G straightforward and to avoid costly mistakes.

In the case of simple buildings, Approved Document G to the Building Regulations provides solutions and performance requirements for complying with Part G. More complex situations can be handled by applying the information contained in the references (provided at the end of each section) to the principles given in this guide.

Every effort has been made to ensure the accuracy of the information included in this guide at the time of publication; however, legislation is constantly being revised and updated. Readers will have ultimate responsibility for ensuring that they have taken account of all of the most up-to-date requirements and the appropriate legislation. It has been assumed in the drafting of this guide that design, specification, installation and maintenance will be carried out by appropriately qualified and experienced personnel.

0.2   Layout of the guide

The layout of the guides in this series provides quick access to the essentials, so that they can be identified and assimilated quickly. The following two types of highlighting are used.

 ESSENTIAL

To aid rapid digestion of the key points, boxes like this contain fundamental material and mandatory requirements.

>
> **FOR INFORMATION**
>
> Useful background information and points of interest are in boxes like this.

0.3   Building Regulations

> The Building Regulations apply only to England and Wales; there are separate regulatory systems in place for Scotland and Northern Ireland.
>
> Generally, the Building Regulations are made for specific purposes: health and safety, energy efficiency of buildings and the welfare and convenience of people in and around buildings.
>
> This update of Part G also includes requirements for the protection of the environment by means of providing new requirements for water efficiency in dwellings.
>
> The requirements of Part G are given in later chapters.

Part G and Approved Document G (AD G) of the Building Regulations came into force on 6 April 2010 and set out detailed requirements for water systems in buildings (both hot and cold), which deal with both physical safety (e.g. prevention of scalding) and health, together with limits on water consumption. They also make requirements for the performance and numbers of sanitary facilities, bathrooms and food preparation areas.

0.4   What is new about this edition of Approved Document G?

The 2010 edition represents a complete overhaul of AD G, which had previously been the oldest of the Approved Documents. New requirements have been added and previous requirements have been extended and reordered.

The extent of the changes is reflected in the title of the new edition, 'Sanitation, hot water safety and water efficiency', compared with 'Hygiene' in the 1992 edition.

This edition includes the requirements of Regulation 17K[1] for water efficiency in dwellings. A certificate specifying the calculated potential usage of wholesome water must be provided for the local authority to award a completion certificate.

It now specifies where wholesome water is to be supplied for the purposes of drinking, washing or food preparation. Softened wholesome water can be used for washing but not for drinking or food preparation. For other uses, such as toilet flushing, the use of alternative sources of water (i.e. water that does not come from a mains supply) is permitted as a means of reducing the use of wholesome water.

The safety of hot water systems has been enhanced in this new edition to take account of fatal accidents that have occurred as a direct result of malfunctioning hot water systems; these now also apply to vented hot water systems as well as to unvented systems. There are also new requirements aimed at prevention of scalding from hot water when bathing.

Requirements for the provision of sanitary conveniences and bathrooms have been updated and extended to situations other than dwellings, such as hostels and halls of residence.

A new requirement for sinks to be provided in food preparation areas has been introduced to formalise current good practice.

The provisions on material change of use have been amended to reflect other changes to Part G. Similarly, the relevant provisions of Part G have been extended to greenhouses, small detached buildings and extensions, including conservatories, where a water system is installed.

Competent person self-certification schemes are recognised for work involving hot water systems and for installation of a sanitary convenience, washing facility or bathroom in a dwelling.

0.5   If I am familiar with the old Approved Document G, what bits do I need to read?

Because of the extensive changes, the whole of the document needs to be read.

It should be noted that the numbering of the requirements has also been changed (Table 1).

Table 1
Comparison of 2010 and 1992 requirements

New edition title	Requirement of 2010 edition	Requirement of 1992 edition
Cold water supply	G1	Not included
Water efficiency	G2	Not included
Hot water supply and systems	G3	G3
Sanitary conveniences and washing facilities	G4	G1
Bathrooms	G5	G2
Kitchens and food preparation areas	G6	Not included

0.6 If I am not familiar with previous versions of Approved Document G, what bits do I need to read?

All of it, as the requirements are relevant to virtually every building project.

Part G and Regulation 17K apply to all new buildings, and also where significant alterations are made to an existing hot or cold water system.

It is important to note that other Parts of the Regulations will almost certainly apply to proposed work. For example, moving a bathroom would also have to comply with, amongst others, Part H (drainage), Part F (ventilation), Part P (electrical safety) and Part M (access). Although alterations to existing buildings may not require the work to be notified to Building Control under Part G, if it involves alterations to systems covered by other Parts (such as drainage) the project would become notifiable under the application of that Part.

The work must also comply with all other applicable Parts of the Regulations.

0.7 Reasons for the changes

As part of its regular review process, Communities and Local Government (CLG) recognised that Part G was in need of general updating. The decision to extend the scope to include water efficiency was driven by the need to make provision against the effects of climate change and increased housing supply, and to improve sustainability. More stringent requirements for hot water safety were a response to the financial and social cost of related injuries.

A CLG/Department for Environment, Food and Rural Affairs (Defra) joint consultation in December 2006, *Water Efficiency in New Buildings*, examined ways in which to promote water efficiency in homes. The results of this consultation were used to develop the water efficiency provisions of the new Part G and Regulation 17K, with a requirement for all new homes to have an estimated water consumption of 125 litres per person per day or less.

The reduction in water usage from the current average level of 150 litres per person per day, and of hot water in particular, will also reduce energy consumption and, hence, carbon dioxide emissions.

Water efficiency in homes is also being encouraged by the *Code for Sustainable Homes* (CSH), and the provisions of Part G and Regulation 17K are consistent with the CSH. In particular, they both use the *Water Efficiency Calculator for New Buildings*.

A consultation paper on proposed changes to Part G and AD G that contained draft requirements and guidance was published by CLG in May 2008. A total of 127 responses to the consultation were received, the majority of which were broadly supportive, and an analysis of the responses was published in November 2008.

The draft AD G was further developed using the consultation responses and discussions with the Building Regulations Advisory Committee (BRAC) Working Party, which comprises manufacturers, developers, architects, building control bodies and installers. The 'draft' AD G and Regulation 17K were laid before Parliament on 13 May 2009 and came into force on 6 April 2010, after a delay caused by receipt of a 'detailed opinion' from the European Commission that necessitated some minor changes.

Evolution of the current AD G is shown in Figure 1.

0.8   When do the requirements of Part G apply?

Part G applies to building work, which is defined[2] as including:

- erection and extension of a building;
- provision or extension of a controlled service or fitting;
- material alteration of a building or a controlled service or fitting; or
- material change of use of a building or part of a building.

'Controlled services and fittings' are those on which Part G imposes a requirement and therefore includes:

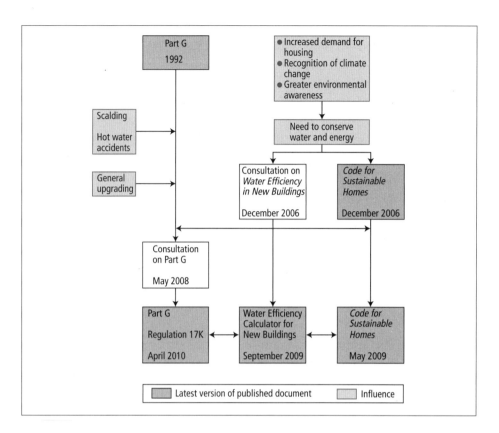

Figure 1
Evolution of Part G

- heating boilers and fuel tanks;
- hot water vessels;
- boiler and hot water storage controls.

Like-for-like replacement of items is generally exempt, but a controlled service that is altered or extended must comply with the requirements of Part G. If a controlled service or fitting did not comply with the requirements of Part G before a building was extended or materially altered, the work must be carried out in such a way that it is no more unsatisfactory than before.

The building must be brought up to the standards required by requirements G1, G3(1) to (3), G4, G5 and G6 where a material change of use[3] takes place. This is where a building:

- is used as a dwelling where previously it was not;
- contains a flat where previously it did not;
- is used as a hotel or boarding house where previously it was not;
- is used as an institution where previously it was not;
- is used as a public building where previously it was not;
- no longer comes within the exemptions in Schedule 2 of the Building Regulations where previously it did;
- which contains at least one dwelling contains a greater or lesser number of dwellings than it did previously;
- contains a room for residential purposes where previously it did not;

- which contains at least one room for residential purposes contains a greater or lesser number of rooms than it did previously;
- is used as a shop where previously it was not.

Buildings that are generally exempt from compliance with the Building Regulations[4] include:

- buildings controlled under other legislation (e.g. buildings in which explosives are manufactured or stored, buildings (other than a building containing a dwelling or a building used for office or canteen accommodation) on nuclear sites, a scheduled ancient monument);
- buildings not frequented by people;
- greenhouses;
- agricultural buildings;
- temporary buildings (i.e. not more than 28 days);
- ancillary buildings (e.g. site huts not used as an office or for sleeping);
- small detached buildings (i.e. less than 30m²) not used as dwellings;
- ground-floor extensions of buildings less than 30m² (e.g. conservatories, porches).

However, cold or hot water systems installed in one of these exempt buildings are still subject to requirement G1 or G3 respectively.

Historic buildings are not exempt from the Building Regulations. However, work on historic buildings should not prejudice the character of the building or increase the risk of long-term deterioration to fabric or fittings. Therefore, common-sense compromise should be exercised in meeting the requirements of Part G whilst maintaining the building's historic qualities.

0.9   Notification of work

Building work should be notified to the building control body (BCB) unless it is carried out by a competent person under a self-certification scheme listed under Schedule 2A,[5] or it is listed in Schedule 2B,[6] which covers:

- in an existing hot water system
  - replacement of a part that is not a combustion appliance
  - addition of an output device or control device, unless commissioning is possible and would affect the reasonable use of fuel and power, e.g. where new water heaters are provided;
- installation of a single stand-alone, self-contained fixed hot water appliance and controls that are not connected to part of any other fixed building service, unless
  - it is a combustion appliance
  - any associated electrical work is notifiable
  - commissioning is possible and would affect the reasonable use of fuel and power, e.g. where new water heaters are provided;
- replacement of a WC or urinal with one that does not use any more water than the one it replaced, or of a washbasin, sink, bidet, bath or shower provided the work does not include any work to:

- – underground drainage
- – hot or cold water systems or above-ground drainage which could prejudice the health and safety of any person on completion of the work;
- replacement of any part or adding an output or control device to an existing cold water system;
- installation of a hot water storage system that has a storage vessel not exceeding 15 litres, provided that any electrical work associated with the installation is also not notifiable and that it is not a combustion appliance or part of another building service (which means that combi boilers are notifiable).

0.10 Competent person schemes

A competent person self-certification scheme allows individuals and enterprises who are competent in their field to self-certify that their work complies with the Building Regulations as an alternative to submitting a building notice or using an approved inspector and thus incurring their fees.

In all schemes, the competent person reports the work to the scheme organiser, who in turn informs the local authority or approved inspector that work has taken place and issues a certificate to the customer. This reporting process must be completed within 30 days of the work being finished.

There are various schemes for work covered by Part G:

i. installation of a hot water service system connected to a heat-producing gas appliance;
ii. installation of a hot water service system connected to an oil-fired combustion appliance;
iii. installation of a hot water service system connected to a solid fuel burning appliance;
iv. installation of a hot water service system connected to an electric heat source;
v. installation of a sanitary convenience, sink, washbasin, bidet, fixed bath, shower or bathroom in a dwelling (not involving work on underground drainage);

vi. installation of a wholesome cold water supply;
vii. installation of a non-wholesome water supply to a sanitary convenience fitted with a flushing device which does not involve work on shared or underground drainage.

Details of the schemes, which are kept under review, including the bodies which assess firms' competence, are given on the CLG website: www.communities.gov.uk/planningandbuilding/buildingregulations/competentpersonsschemes/existingcompetentperson/

0.11 Completion certificates

A completion certificate certifies that the BCB[7] is satisfied that the work complies with the relevant requirements of the Building Regulations, in so far as it has been possible to ascertain this. For this reason, it is very important that the BCB is called in to inspect various stages of work as it progresses.

Where only non-notifiable work is carried out, there is no requirement for a certificate to be given.

A completion certificate is a valuable document, as it may be difficult to sell the building without it. Completion certificates are not available if work is carried out under a 'building notice'.

Notes

1. Regulation 17K of the Building Regulations 2000 (as amended).
2. Regulation 3 of the Building Regulations 2000.
3. Regulation 5 of the Building Regulations 2000.
4. Regulation 9 of the Building Regulations 2000 (as amended).
5. Schedule 2A to the Building Regulations 2000 (as amended).
6. Schedule 2B to the Building Regulations 2000 (as amended).
7. A local authority or an approved inspector.

Cold water supply (G1)

1.1   The requirement

> **COLD WATER SUPPLY**
>
> **G1**
> (1)   There must be a suitable installation for the provision of:
>   (a)   wholesome water to any place where drinking water is drawn off;
>   (b)   wholesome water or softened wholesome water to any washbasin or bidet provided in or adjacent to a room containing a sanitary convenience;
>   (c)   wholesome water or softened wholesome water to any washbasin, bidet, fixed bath and shower in a bathroom; and
>   (d)   wholesome water to any sink provided in any area where food is prepared.
> (2)   There must be a suitable installation for the provision of water of suitable quality to any sanitary convenience fitted with a flushing device.
>
> **Limits on application**
> None.

1.2   How does this fit in with other regulations?

Regulation 22 of the Workplace (Health, Safety and Welfare) Regulations 1992 requires 'an adequate supply of wholesome drinking water' to be provided, which is 'readily accessible' to all staff in workplaces. Drinking water should normally be obtained from a public or private water supply by means of a tap on a pipe connected directly to the water main. Alternatively, drinking water may be derived from a tap on a pipe connected directly to a storage cistern that complies with the requirements of the Water Regulations, and is kept clean and tested and disinfected as necessary. Water should be provided in refillable closed containers only where it cannot be obtained directly from a mains supply, although bottled water/water dispensing systems may still be provided as a secondary source of drinking water. In addition, as far as is reasonably practicable, drinking water taps should not be installed in sanitary accommodation or in places where contamination is likely. Further details of these regulations are given in Chapter 4.

The Water Supply (Water Fittings) Regulations 1999[1] (often referred to as the Water Regulations) also include requirements to prevent:

- contamination;
- waste;
- undue consumption;
- erroneous measurement;
- misuse of water.

(In this context, 'misuse' means to take water without paying for it.)

Detailed guidance on compliance with the Water Regulations is given in the *Water Regulations Guide*.

There are two reasons why a new Regulation G1 has been introduced for cold water systems even though they are already covered by the Water Regulations:

1. to ensure the health of building users through the supply of wholesome water to all buildings (the Water Regulations cover only those supplied by the public water supply); and
2. stating those applications where wholesome water is required introduces the possibility of using water of a lesser quality for other applications, such as garden watering, toilet flushing and, possibly, laundry.

1.3 When is water wholesome?

'Wholesome' water is fit to use for drinking, cooking, food preparation or washing without any potential danger to human health by meeting the requirements of regulations made under Section 67 (Standards of Wholesomeness) of the Water Act 1991. These stipulate the criteria that the water must meet in order to protect the lifelong health of the population. These parameters include limits on:

- biological quality (including levels of bacteria and oocysts);
- chemical quality (including levels of metals, solvents, pesticides and hydrocarbons);
- physical qualities (including colour, taste and odour).

The quality of water that is supplied through public water mains is strictly controlled by legislation[2] to ensure that it is wholesome, and is also subject to regular testing at the consumer's tap to prevent any loss of quality during transmission and storage.

Water supplied through the mains is wholesome.

Water that is supplied from private sources is subject to similar quality requirements[3] and therefore is also considered to be wholesome.

Within premises, water systems are subject to Water Regulations[1] in order to prevent contamination of the water once it has left the water supplier's mains.

G1 lists those applications for which wholesome water must be supplied:

- drinking;
- food preparation.

In very hard water areas, ion exchange water softeners can increase sodium levels above the permitted limit for wholesome water (200 mg Na/litre). Because of the potential health implications to infants, and people on a low-salt diet or with other medical conditions, this water should not be used for drinking or food preparation. However, G1 considers softened wholesome water to be suitable for washing (i.e. washbasins, baths, showers and bidets) or for toilet and urinal flushing as an alternative to wholesome water. This is consistent with the *Water Regulations Guide*, which advises that a water softener should be fitted after the draw-off to a drinking water tap.

For some purposes, for example toilet flushing, water that is less than wholesome can be used. The quality of the water that can be used is dependent upon its end use, and therefore the appropriate quality needs to be assessed on the basis of risk. For example, water used for toilet flushing can be of relatively poor quality, as there is negligible personal contact with the water and the water in the WC bowl is already contaminated. Similarly, the quality of water used for garden watering with a watering can does not need to be high, but consideration should be given to water quality where plants for human consumption are grown. On the other hand, water that could come into contact with people, either directly or as an aerosol, presents a higher risk and therefore needs to be of better quality; for example, water delivered by high-pressure hoses used for vehicle washing, as well as potentially contaminating people, will give off an aerosol, and so presents a significant risk of *Legionella*. It should be noted that because larger systems have the potential to affect the health of a greater number of people, they should incorporate greater protection than that for a single dwelling.

There is some debate as to whether or not the water used for washing clothes needs to be wholesome. Recent research in Australia[4] indicates that highly treated recycled water (intended for machine washing of clothes) will not lead to the transmission of micro-organisms in numbers likely to cause enteric diseases.

Alternative sources of non-wholesome include:

- groundwater abstracted from boreholes, wells or springs;
- surface water from watercourses (e.g. streams, brooks, rivers) or ponds and lakes;
- rainwater (generally collected and stored, referred to as 'harvested rainwater');
- greywater (i.e. wastewater from baths, basins and showers);
- treated wastewater (from sewage treatment plants or industrial processes).

The quality of the water from each of these sources will be different, and even from a single source will vary over time.

If an alternative water source is being considered, its reliability to provide the necessary quantity of water should also be assessed. Where the quantity cannot be guaranteed (excluding exceptional events, as even water mains can burst and cause cuts), a back-up supply will be needed. If the back-up supply is from a wholesome water source, there must be no possibility of contamination of the wholesome water supply by non-wholesome water (by strict compliance with the Water Regulations).

It is essential that non-wholesome water is not inadvertently supplied instead of wholesome water nor allowed to contaminate wholesome water systems. Prevention of contamination can be assured by compliance with the Water Regulations. (It should be noted that water can be drawn into wholesome water systems by partial vacuums, even being sucked through the air where there is an insufficient gap between the water and the pipework.) Inadvertent mis-connections can be avoided by clear and unambiguous marking of non-wholesome pipes and cisterns; using different types of pipework for wholesome and alternative water systems can also help to avoid mis-connections (e.g. copper for wholesome and plastics for non-wholesome), but marking is still essential, especially if the pipes are insulated. It should be noted that there are standard colours for different services (e.g. yellow for gas), with blue being assigned to water mains, so blue pipes should not be used for non-wholesome water.

Inside dwellings, labels should be used to identify non-wholesome pipework. Labels should be:

- green in accordance with BS 4800:1989 colour 12 D 45;
- not less than 100mm long;
- marked 'NON-WHOLESOME WATER' in black letters not less than 5mm high (note that other guides recommend different wording, such as 'Reclaimed water', 'Non-potable water' or 'Rainwater' – any term may be used provided that the message is clear);
- self-adhesive, wrap-around or mechanically fixed to the pipe at intervals not greater than 500mm and at key connection points.

For large-scale reclaimed water pipelines (e.g. multi-occupancy buildings, schools, offices) and where the pipes are insulated, marking in accordance with the principles of BS 1710 should be used, as shown in Figure 2.

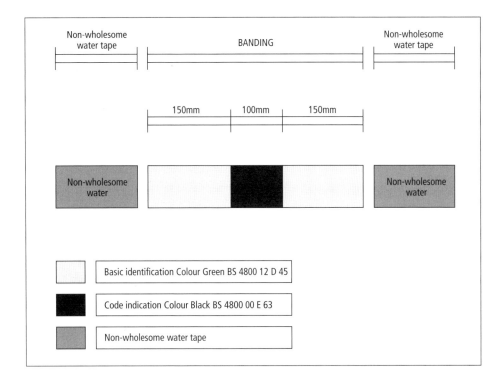

Figure 2
Non-wholesome water pipe marking

Points of use should also be clearly identified by a label stating 'Non-wholesome water' or by a prohibition sign.

If, after a risk assessment, an alternative source of water is used, it is essential that the system is properly inspected and maintained so that it continues to supply the quality and quantity of water as intended. These routine checks should include:

- sources (e.g. check that there is no obvious contamination of the source);
- storage systems (check for contamination, e.g. a dead bird, in the storage cistern);
- filters (e.g. that they are not blocked or holed);
- treatment (e.g. by checking water quality);
- pumps (e.g. check electrical safety);
- distribution pipework (e.g. check that there are no leaks or mis-connections).

Further details of rainwater harvesting systems are given in BS 8515:2009. Other British Standards are in preparation covering re-use of effluent from wastewater treatment plants and greywater re-use system.

1.4 'Sufficient' pressure and flow

Static pressure at any point in a system is the height to which water would rise if there were no flow. As soon as water flows in a system, pressure losses will occur as a result of resistance in the pipes and fittings (e.g. valves, bends and tees), so the water will not rise so far. This is referred to as the dynamic pressure and is illustrated in Figure 3.

The system must be designed in such a way that there is sufficient pressure to operate the sanitary appliance properly. The pressure is limited to the height either of the cold water storage cistern or the pressure in the main to which the appliance is connected. The losses in the pipework are related to the flow of water, the length and size of pipework and the number of fittings; a calculation method is given in Annex D of BS 6700:2006+A1:2009.

In the case of outlets (i.e. taps etc.) designed to be supplied from a cistern, the dynamic pressure at the outlet should be at least 0.5m head of water. For outlets designed to be supplied directly from the mains, the dynamic pressure should be that recommended by the manufacturer of the outlet.

The system design and specification of outlets should provide flow rates as given in Table 2 (based upon Table 3 of BS 6700:2006+A1:2009).

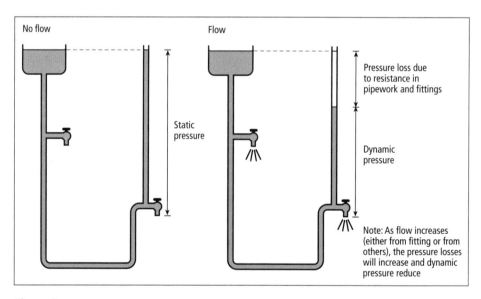

Figure 3
Pressure and flow rate

Table 2
Flow rates

Outlet fitting	Rate of flow (l/s)		Comment
	Design rate	Minimum rate	
WC cistern	0.13	0.05	To fill in 2 minutes
Washbasin	0.15	0.10	
Handbasin (pillar taps)	0.10	0.07	
Handbasin (spray or spray mixing taps)	0.05	0.03	
Bidet	0.20	0.10	
Bath (¾-inch taps)	0.30	0.20	
Bath (1-inch taps)	0.60	0.40	
Shower head	0.20	0.10	Check with manufacturer
Kitchen sink (½-inch taps)	0.20	0.10	
Kitchen sink (¾-inch taps)	0.30	0.20	
Washing machine	0.20	0.15	Check with manufacturer
Dishwasher	0.15	0.10	Check with manufacturer
Urinal cistern (each position served)	0.004	0.002	
Urinal flushing cisterns	0.3 maximum	0.15 minimum	

1.5 Relevant British Standards and other guidance

Reference	Publisher	Obtain and read?
BS 6700:2006+A1:2009 *Design, installation, testing and maintenance of services supplying water for domestic use within buildings and their curtilages*	BSI	Essential
Water Regulations Guide	Water Research Centre (WRc)	Essential
Water Fittings and Materials Directory (www.wras.co.uk/Directory)	Water Regulations Advisory Service (WRAS)	Preferable Essential for detailed design and specification
BS 8515:2009 *Rainwater harvesting systems – Code of practice*	BSI	Essential if rainwater harvesting used
BS 8535 *Reuse of wastewater from treatment plants* Part 1. *Water reuse for outdoor use* Part 2. *Water reuse for irrigation* Part 3. *Water reuse for community schemes* Part 4. *Water reuse for commercial property*	BSI – in preparation	
BS 8525 *Greywater reuse systems.* Part 1. *Code of practice for installation* Part 2. *Performance test procedures*	BSI – in preparation	

Notes

1. The Water Supply (Water Fittings) Regulations 1999 (SI 1999/1148).
2. For England, the Water Supply (Water Quality) Regulations 2000 (SI 2000/3184 as amended), and for Wales the Water Supply (Water Quality) Regulations 2001 (SI 2001/3911 as amended).
3. For England, the Private Water Supplies Regulations 2009 (SI 2009/3101), and for Wales the Private Water Supplies (Wales) Regulations 2010 (SI 2010/66).
4. Joanne O'Toole, Karin Leder, Martha Sinclair (2008) *A Series of Exposure Experiments – Recycled Water and Alternative Water Sources. Part B: Microbial Transfer Efficiency During Machine Clothes and Microbial Survival Turf-Grass Experiments.* Research Report No. 46, Department of Epidemiology and Preventive Medicine, Monash University, Australia.

Water efficiency (G2 and Regulation 17K)

2.1 The requirement

WATER EFFICIENCY

Water efficiency

G2

Reasonable provision must be made by the installation of fittings and fixed appliances that use water efficiently for the prevention of undue consumption of water.

Water efficiency of new dwellings

Regulation 17K

(1) The potential consumption of wholesome water by persons occupying a dwelling to which this regulation applies should not exceed 125 litres per person per day, calculated in accordance with the methodology set out in the document *The Water Efficiency Calculator for New Dwellings.*

(2) This regulation applies to a dwelling which is:
   (a) erected; or
   (b) formed by a material change of use of a building within the meaning of Regulations 5(a) or (b).

Wholesome water consumption calculation

20E. – (1) Where Regulation 17K applies, the person carrying out the work must give the local authority a notice which specifies the potential consumption of wholesome water per person per day calculated in accordance with the methodology referred to in that regulation in relation to the completed dwelling.

(2) The notice shall be given to the local authority not later than five days after the work has been completed.

Building (Approved Inspector) Regulations 2000

12E. (1)   Where Regulation 17K of the Principal Regulations applies to work which is the subject of an initial notice, the person carrying out the work must give the Approved Inspector a notice which specifies the potential consumption of wholesome water per person per day calculated in accordance with the methodology referred to in that regulation in relation to the completed dwelling.

(2)   The notice shall be given to the Approved Inspector not later than:

(a)   five days after the work has been completed; or

(b)   the date on which, in accordance with Regulation 18, the initial notice ceases to be in force,

whichever is the earlier.

Limits on application
Requirement G2 applies only when a dwelling is:

(a)   erected; or

(b)   formed by a material change of use of a building within the meaning of Regulation 5(a) or (b).

Regulation 17K is consistent with the requirement of the *Code for Sustainable Homes* (CSH) in setting a maximum calculated water consumption of 120 litres per person per day within the home. However, because building regulations apply to premises (i.e. to gardens as well as to buildings), there is an additional allowance of 5 litres per person per day for external uses such as garden watering or car washing.

The external allowance applies even to homes without a garden (e.g. flats) as there are still likely to be associated external uses, such as watering and cleaning communal grounds and parking areas.

Calculated wholesome water consumption shall be not greater than 125 litres per person per day in dwellings.

The Water Efficiency Calculator has been developed as a simplified method that can be used for comparison of different homes. Calculations provided for G2 will also satisfy CSH and Home Information Packs (HIPs).

WHY 125 LITRES PER PERSON PER DAY?

Government policy on improving water efficiency overall, and in new buildings in particular, is contained in the joint Defra/CLG policy statement[1] of July 2007. This was prompted by scarcity of water during the drought of 2004–06 and an increasing awareness that:

- water resources are vulnerable to prolonged dry spells;
- climate change models suggest that drought events will occur more frequently;
- water demand will continue to grow as a result of increases in population, numbers of households and water use per person;
- environmental limits are close to being exceeded, and there is a risk that environmental standards set by European legislation, such as the Water Framework and Habitats Directives, will not be met;
- reducing water consumption will reduce energy usage (and hence CO_2 emissions);
- reducing water consumption (assuming that the total of wholesome and non-wholesome water use reduces) will reduce sewer flows and treated wastewater discharges.

The average consumption of water per person in England and Wales in 2005/06 was around 150 litres per day. Average household demand has increased by around 55% over the last 25 years and continues to increase at 1% per annum.

Therefore, after consultation, government policy is to reduce domestic water consumption (i.e. water used for drinking, food preparation, washing and toilet flushing) by:

- requiring new homes to have a maximum calculated wholesome water consumption of 125 litres per person per day (implemented through the Building Regulations);
- setting performance-based standards for individual types of water fittings such as toilets, taps and showers (implemented through the Water Regulations).

A maximum calculated water consumption of 125 litres per person per day was chosen as it is:

- a very significant improvement on current water use (present average consumption per person in metered properties including external water use is around 135 litres per person per day);
- equivalent to 120 litres per person per day of level 1 of the CSH (plus an allowance of 5 litres per person per day for external water use);
- regarded as being challenging but achievable by using the best fittings that are currently readily available.

Care should be taken to use the September 2009 edition (or later amendments) of the calculator, as it was altered from the May 2009 version to make it easier to achieve the 125 litres per person per day limit.

It should be noted that the actual water consumption may be more or less than the calculated demand because it is determined by user behaviour (e.g. length of time spent in the home, the length of time spent showering, the number of WC flushes). However, the calculator does give the same result as the current average consumption of 150 litres per day and so the maximum 125 litres per day should result in an overall 17% water saving in new dwellings.

The calculator allows different choices to be made as long as the maximum allowance is not exceeded. For example, baths and power showers can be used but their consumption must be offset by, for example, the installation of an alternative source of water for toilet flushing.

To use the calculator, it is necessary to compile water consumption figures from manufacturers' data for each terminal fitting to be used.

Logic diagrams for using the calculator are given in Figure 4. A worked example is given in the Appendix.

WRc has developed an online version of the calcualtor, which can be found at www.wrcplc.co.uk/partcalculator/Default.aspx. It is anticipated that this version will be populated with data for fittings from different manaufacturers in due course. Advice on saving water is given on the Waterwise website: www.waterwise.org.uk.

The sanitary appliances and white goods used in the calculator must be provided and installed.

Any alternative sources of water used in the calculator must be installed.

A record, together with sufficient other information to allow proper maintenance in order to preserve the water efficiency of the building, must be provided to the building owner or occupier of:

- the sanitary appliances and white goods used to meet the target (as used in the calculator);
- any alternative water sources.

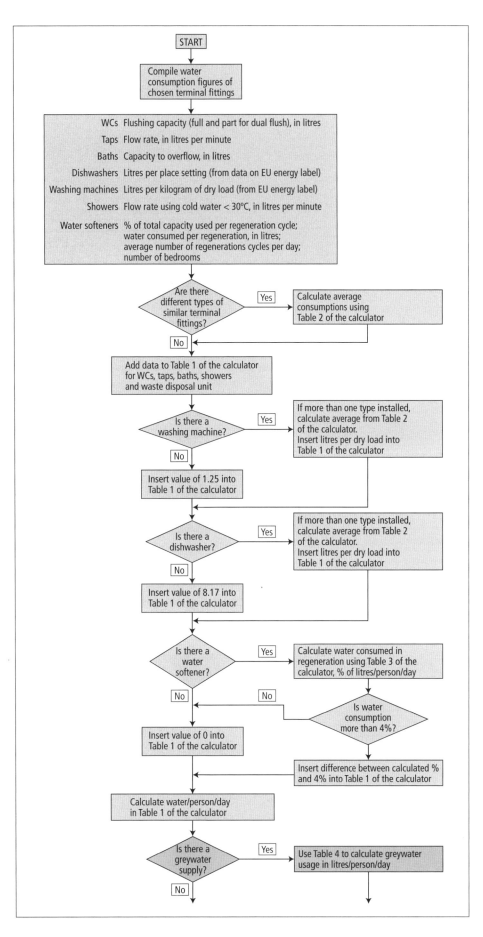

Figure 4
Logic diagram showing use of the calculator

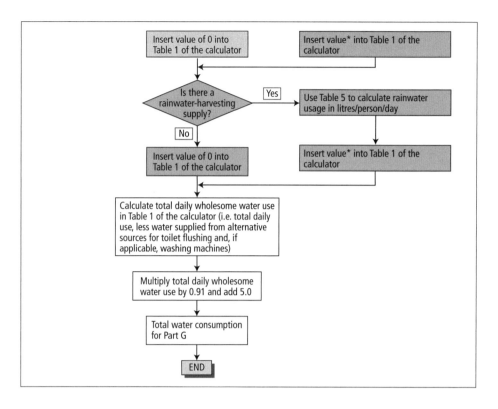

Figure 4
Continued

*Note that value cannot be greater than calculated usage for flushing.

2.2   Notices

> A notice specifying the calculated wholesome water
> consumption in litres per person per day relating to the
> dwelling must be given to the appropriate building control
> body, normally not later than five days after the completion of
> the building work.
>
> A final certificate cannot be given without receipt of the
> notice.[2]

2.3   Relevant British Standards and other guidance

Reference	Publisher	Obtain and read?
The Water Efficiency Calculator for New Dwellings September 2009 (or later) edition	CLG	Essential

Notes

1. 'Water efficiency in new buildings', a joint Defra and *Communities and Local Government* policy statement, July 2007.
2. Under Regulation 20E of the Building Regulations 2000 (as amended) for local authorities or Regulation 12E of the Building (Approved Inspectors etc.) Regulations 2000 for approved inspectors.

Hot water supply and systems (G3)

3.1 The requirement

HOT WATER SUPPLY AND SYSTEMS

G3

(1) There must be a suitable installation for the provision of heated wholesome water or heated softened wholesome water to:

   (a) any washbasin or bidet provided in or adjacent to a room containing a sanitary convenience;

   (b) any washbasin, bidet, fixed bath and shower in a bathroom; and

   (c) any sink provided in any area where food is prepared.

(2) A hot water system, including any cistern or other vessel that supplies water to or receives expansion water from a hot water system, shall be designed, constructed and installed so as to resist the effects of temperature and pressure that may occur either in normal use or in the event of such malfunctions as may reasonably be anticipated, and must be adequately supported.

(3) A hot water system that has a hot water storage vessel shall incorporate precautions to:

   (a) prevent the temperature of the water stored in the vessel at any time exceeding 100°C; and

   (b) ensure that any discharge from safety devices is safely conveyed to where it is visible but will not cause a danger to persons in or about the building.

(4) The hot water supply to any fixed bath must be so designed and installed as to incorporate measures to ensure that the temperature of the water that can be delivered to that bath shall not exceed 48°C.

Limits on application

Requirement G3(3) does not apply to a system which heats or stores water for the purposes only of an industrial process.

Requirement G3(4) applies only when a dwelling is:

(a)   erected;
(b)   formed by a material change of use within the meaning of Regulation 5(a) or (b).

Heated water must be supplied from a wholesome cold water supply (e.g. mains) and comply with the Water Supply (Water Fittings) Regulations 1999. It may be softened.

Heated wholesome water must be supplied to:

- washbasins provided in association with sanitary conveniences;
- washbasins, showers, baths and bidets in bathrooms in dwellings or rooms for residential purposes;
- sinks in food preparation areas.

Heated wholesome water used for food preparation, cooking, cleaning or personal washing is referred to as 'domestic hot water'. The definition refers only to the use of water, not to where it is used.

The use of alternative sources of water for heated water for food preparation and for washing people and utensils (i.e. in sinks, washbasins, baths, showers, bidets and dishwashers) is not permitted, although softened wholesome water is.

It should be noted that the requirement of G3 to supply heated water applies only to the sanitary appliances in bathrooms, toilets and food preparation areas, but does not preclude supplying heated wholesome water to other sinks (including cleaners' sinks), washbasins, baths, showers, bidets, washing machines and dishwashers.

The domestic hot water system should be designed, installed, operated and maintained in such a way that hot water is delivered without waste, misuse or undue consumption of water. This can be achieved by complying with the *Water Regulations Guide* and BS 6700:2006+A1:2009. Other regulations and guides are shown in Table 3.

To avoid wasting water, the system should be designed either to minimise the transfer time between the hot water storage system and hot water outlets or have a circulation system, with short lengths of pipework between the circulating hot water and the outlets.

Table 3
Other regulations associated with hot water systems

Associated area		Regulation	Specifications/guides
Water		Water Supply (Water Fittings) Regulations 1999	BS 6700:2006+A1:2009 *Specification for design, installation, testing and maintenance of services supplying water for domestic use within buildings and their curtilages*
			Water Regulations Guide
			BS EN 12897:2006 *Water supply. Specification for indirectly heated unvented (closed) storage heaters*
Electricity		BS 7671:2008 *Requirements for electrical installations* (IEE Wiring Regulations 17th Edition)	
		Building Regulations 2000 Schedule 1 Part P (Electrical safety – Dwellings)	Approved Document P
Gas		Gas Safety (Installation and Use) Regulations	
Safety	For workplaces	*Legionnaires' Disease: Control of Legionella Bacteria in Water Systems*. Approved Code of Practice and guidance, L8. Health and Safety Commission, 2000	
	For hot water systems used solely for supplying hot water for industrial purposes	Pressure Systems Safety Regulations 2000	*Safety of Pressure Systems. Pressure Systems Safety Regulations 2000.* Approved Code of Practice, L122. HSE Books, 2000

3.2　Different types of domestic water heating systems

There are a large number of different methods of providing heated water for domestic use. However, these can be divided into three basic categories:

- instantaneous;
- water-jacketed tube heaters or thermal stores;
- storage, either:
  - vented
  - unvented.

These are briefly described below but it should be noted that, because there are so many configurations available, it is not possible to do more than provide an overview here. Specialist advice should be sought when choosing, designing, installing or maintaining a hot water system.

A comparison of the different types of water heaters is given in Table 4.

3.2.1   Instantaneous

The simplest systems are instantaneous water heaters, in which cold water is directly heated by either electricity or gas as it passes through a heat exchanger. The heat source is controlled automatically by the flow of water.

Instantaneous heaters can supply hot water to either several outlets (e.g. taps) or a single outlet (e.g. a shower). In the case of instantaneous water heaters that store 15 litres or less, no expansion vessel is needed, provided that there is at least a 3m length of incoming pipework before any valve.

Typical instantaneous heaters are illustrated in Figure 5.

3.2.2   Thermal stores

A thermal store is a tank of water that is heated by a boiler, an immersion heater or solar panels. The body of water within the thermal store is used purely as a medium for storing heat, acting like a battery for heat. The heat of the stored water is transferred to cold water as it passes through a heat exchanger (there is no direct contact or mixing between the hot water and the water inside the thermal store).

The cold water supply is normally at mains pressure, providing hot water at mains pressure.

Thermal stores can be either unvented (with the contents being manually topped up as necessary from the mains) or vented (with the contents being automatically topped up from the cold water cistern. Unvented stores need to be fitted with an expansion vessel (except where their capacity is 15 litres or less and expansion can be accommodated in the cold water supply pipework) and appropriate safety devices. A typical vented thermal store is illustrated in Figure 6.

Table 4
Comparison of hot water supply and storage systems

Type of system	Advantages	Disadvantages
Instantaneous	Heats water only when needed, saving energy Small Few restrictions on location (gas regulations apply) Vented or unvented cold water supply Unlimited quantity of hot water No need for a hot water storage cylinder	Relatively low flow rate, typically 8 to 16 litres/minute Suitable only for relatively small installations, unless several are used to supply different locations Most efficient when one tap is used at a time Likely pressure and flow drop when other taps are opened Relatively high power demand, requiring an adequate electricity or gas supply
Thermal store	Hot water can be either at mains pressure (avoiding the need for a cold water cistern) or from a cold water cistern (providing continuity of supply during water cuts) Reasonably large quantity of hot water, up to around 40 litres/minute No pipework or cold water cisterns needed in roof space (eliminating risk from frost) Reasonable flow rate, up to 25 litres/minute No scaling No risk of *Legionella* contamination	*Unvented thermal stores* Safety devices must be fitted and maintained Discharge pipework from safety devices must be routed through building *Vented thermal stores* Space required for cold water cistern Cold water cisterns and pipework needed in roof space (subject to risks from frost)
Vented stored water	Provides a reasonably large quantity of hot water Good flow rates Fewer safety devices needed than with an unvented system Cold water cistern provides continuity of supply during water cuts In properly designed systems, opening other taps has little effect on flow and pressure Smaller mains can be used	Space required for cold water cistern Cold water cisterns and pipework needed in roof space (subject to risks from frost) Relatively low pressure Where cold draw-off points (taps, showers, etc.) are not supplied from the cold water cistern, pressure will be unbalanced. Filling noise Potential entry point for contamination Potential risk of *Legionella* contamination

Table 4
Continued

Type of system	Advantages	Disadvantages
Unvented stored water	Reasonably large quantity of hot water Reasonable flow rates Balanced pressure in hot and cold water draw-off points (taps, showers, etc.) No pipework or cold water cisterns needed in roof space (eliminating risks from frost) No risk of *Legionella* contamination	Safety devices must be fitted and maintained Discharge pipework from safety devices must be routed through building Larger mains needed Pressure and flow dependent upon mains pressure
Combi boiler	Only single boiler needed, saving space and pipework Heats water only when needed, saving energy Small Single packaged unit reduces site work Few restrictions on location (gas regulations apply) Unlimited quantity of hot water No need for cisterns in the roof space, no hot water storage cylinder and associated pipework	Suitable only for relatively small installations Relatively low flow rate, typically 8 to 16 litres/minute Most efficiently when one tap is used at a time Relatively high power demand, requiring an adequate electricity or gas supply Noise of filling Relatively short life Failure affects both hot water and space heating
Combination tanks	Save space No need for cistern or pipework in roof space, avoiding freezing risks Balanced hot and cold draw-off points (taps, showers, etc.) Separate cold water cistern not required	Limited storage capacity Poor water pressure
Solar systems	Reduced use of fossil fuels	Correctly orientated space needed for solar collectors Uncontrolled temperatures in solar circuit (–20°C to over 130°C)
Heat pumps	Reduced use of fossil fuel Controllable	Relatively low heat Relatively high capital cost

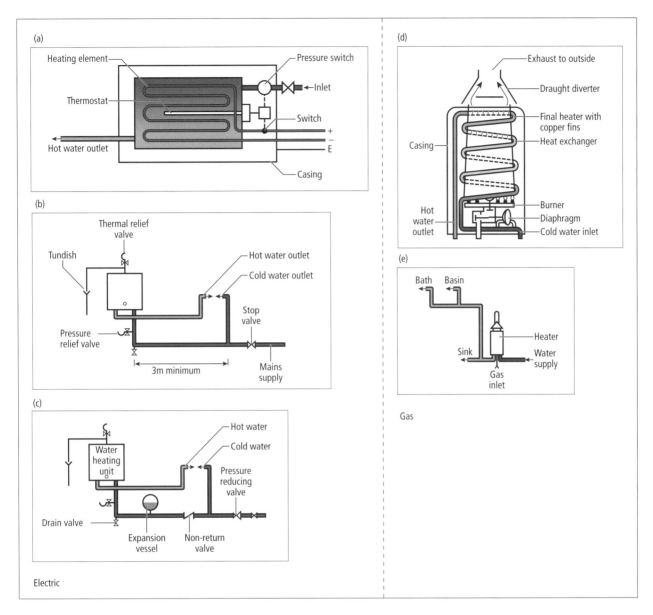

Figure 5
Typical instantaneous water heaters. (a) Typical instantaneous electric water heater (to BSEN 60335-2-35). (b) Installation of unvented hot water units of less than 15 litres capacity. (c) Alternative installation of unvented hot water unit. (d) Typical instantaneous gas water heater. (e) Installation of instantaneous gas water heater. Adapted from a diagram on pp59 and 61 of *Building Services Handbook,* 4th edn, by Fred Hall and Roger Greeno (published by Elsevier, 2007)

3.2.3   Vented stored hot water systems

Cold water from a cold water cistern is fed into a cylinder, which has a vent pipe of at least 19mm internal diameter from the top of the cylinder rising continuously to a predetermined height above the cold feed cistern and discharging through the cover. (Copper pipes are designated by their external diameter, which is 22mm for an internal diameter of 19mm.)

In direct systems, the water in the cylinder is heated directly by passing through a boiler or by using an immersion heater. This is illustrated in Figure 7. Direct systems should not be used in hard water areas because of the build-up of scale, which can block pipes between the boiler and cylinder, or where the same boiler supplies both the central heating and the domestic hot water.

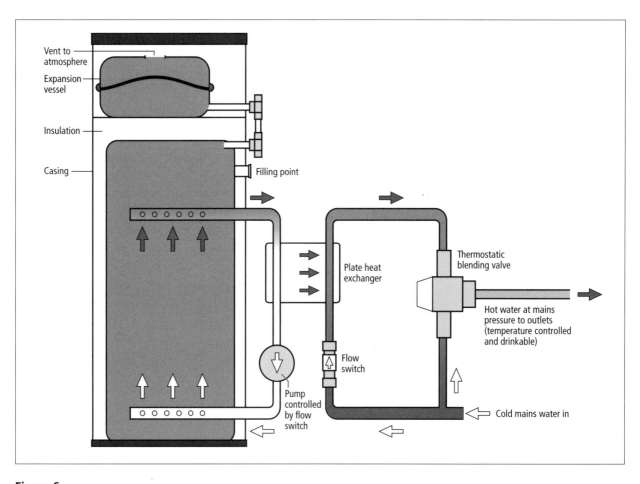

Figure 6
Typical thermal store. © www.plumbworld.co.uk

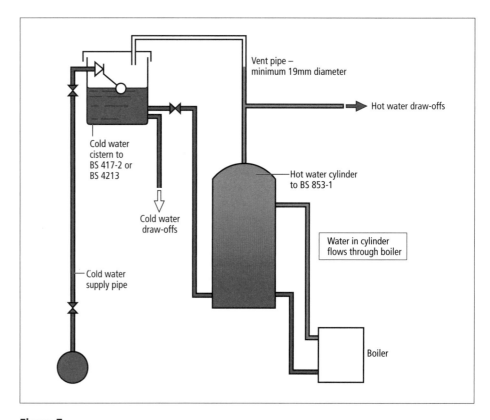

Figure 7
Typical direct vented hot water system. Note: safety devices not shown for clarity. © BSI

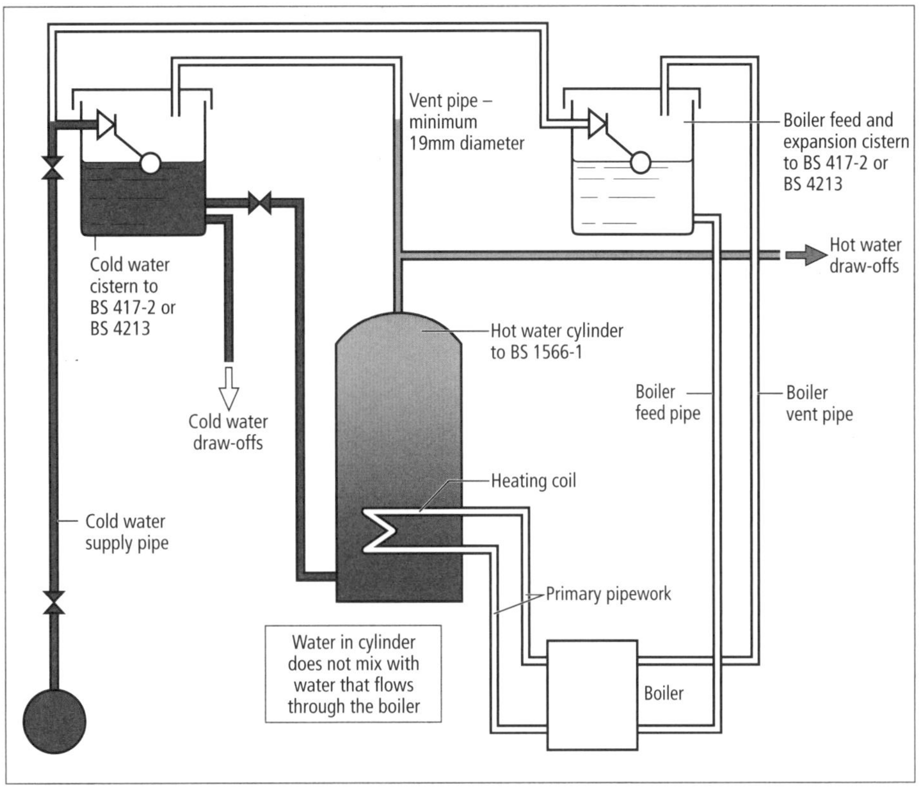

Figure 8
Typical indirect vented hot water system. Note: safety devices not shown for clarity. © BSI

In indirect systems (the more normal arrangement for vented systems), hot water from the boiler circulates through a coil of pipework within the cylinder to heat the domestic hot water; the hot water from the boiler does not mix with the domestic hot water in the cylinder. This is illustrated in Figure 8. An immersion heater can be used in hot water cylinders in either direct or indirect systems.

Hot water cylinders can be either double feed or single feed. In double-feed indirect cylinders (the more usual situation), hot water from the boiler (referred to as 'primary water') circulates through a coil of pipework in the cylinder to heat the domestic hot water. Single-feed indirect cylinders incorporate an air pocket to prevent the primary water mixing with the domestic hot water.

Combination-type storage cylinders incorporate the cold water feed cistern on top of the hot water cylinder, as illustrated in Figure 9. This type of storage cylinder must be installed at a high enough level to give adequate flow at the outlets.

3.2.4 Unvented stored hot water systems

Unvented storage cylinders are supplied with cold water directly from the mains and do not have permanent venting. Figure 10 illustrates the components of an unvented domestic hot water system.

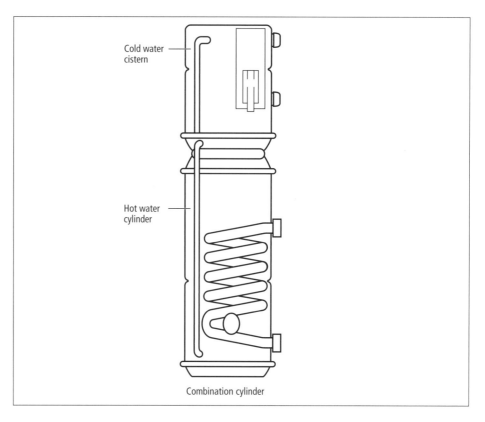

Figure 9
Combination cylinder. © www.plumbworld.co.uk

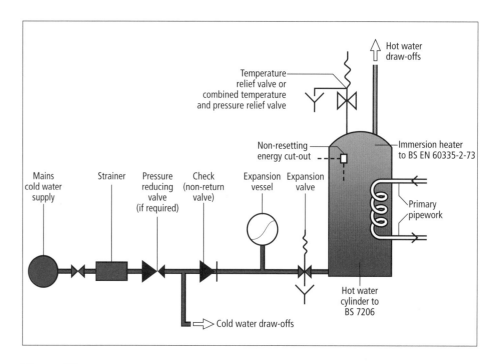

Figure 10
Schematic of typical unvented hot water storage system. Note these components should normally be supplied as a factory-made unit or package.

As there is no vent to relieve any build-up of pressure caused by thermal expansion of water, additional safety devices are needed to prevent bursting or explosion. It is essential that these devices are properly maintained.

Systems storing less than 500 litres of hot water should be supplied as a proprietary package with all the ancillary safety equipment fitted and pre-set at the factory. The components included with the cylinder are shown in Figure 10.

3.2.5   Combi boilers

The 'combi' gas boiler functions both as an instantaneous domestic hot water heater and also as the central heating boiler. A typical installation is illustrated in Figure 11.

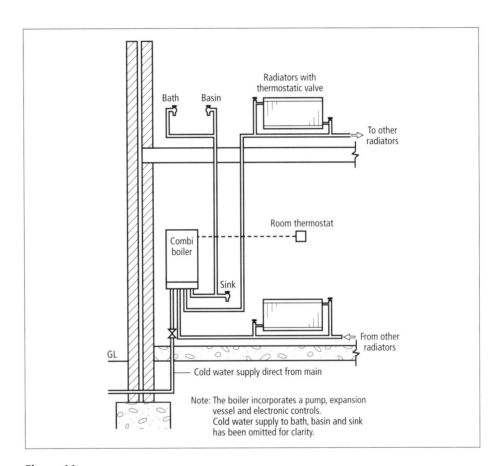

Figure 11
Typical combi boiler. Adapted from a diagram on p54 of *Building Services Handbook,* 4th edn, by Fred Hall and Roger Greeno (published by Elsevier, 2007)

3.2.6   Solar water heating

Solar energy may be used to supplement a conventional domestic water heating system, although in hot sunny weather solar energy alone may be sufficient to heat water to the required draw-off temperatures.

Many different designs of solar water heating systems are possible, from simple direct-feed gravity systems to more complex pumped circuits using two indirect storage cylinders or one cylinder with two indirect coils.

However, the most common form uses an indirect primary circuit which isolates the solar heat transfer fluid from the domestic hot water.

The most common heat exchanger is a coil located within the secondary water storage, although external plate exchangers, in which the primary fluid passes in a 'jacket' surrounding the hot water cylinder walls, can also be used.

The solar primary circuit is generally independent from other circuits, in order to avoid problems of circulating heat generated from fossil fuels to the solar collector, protection from freezing and incompatibility of corrosion inhibitors.

A typical arrangement is shown in Figure 12.

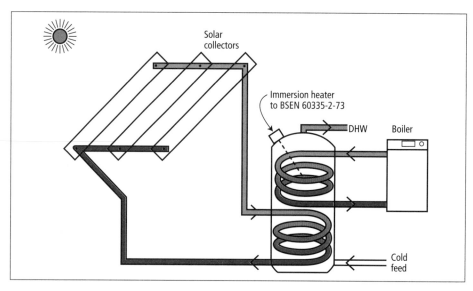

Figure 12
Simplified schematic of a typical solar-heated hot water storage system. Notes: (1) cylinders may be either vented or unvented; (2) solar system may be either vented or unvented; (3) many variations exist. ©The Domestic Building Services Panel of CIBSE. (Pre-heating domestic hot water system illustrated.)

3.2.7 Heat pumps

A heat pump is, in principle, a refrigeration cycle in reverse, extracting heat from a low-temperature source and upgrading it to a higher temperature for heat emission or water heating. The low-temperature heat source may be water, air or soil.

Some heat pump systems are able to heat domestic hot water through a modern high-efficiency indirect water cylinder. An immersion heater can then boost the temperature, which can be done at night using off-peak tariffs.

3.3   Safety requirements

TRAGEDIES CAUSED BY FAILURE OF HOT WATER SYSTEMS

Rhianna Hardie, who was just 10 months old, died after a thermostat failed and boiling water cascaded from a tank in the attic into the room below, where she was asleep, on 19 November 2006. She suffered 95% burns and died three weeks later.

This was caused by failure of the thermostat in an immersion heater, which then heated up water in a poorly supported cold water cistern that became weakened by the heat, distorted and then split.

This was very similar to the circumstances that caused the death of Sharon Minster, 41, in May 2002. She suffered 45% burns and died nine days later.

Lessons learnt from these two, thankfully rare, incidents have been incorporated into this edition of Part G to prevent any recurrence.

Hot water systems must be designed to be safe during normal use and malfunction.

All hot water systems should be designed, installed, commissioned and maintained in such a way that they do not present a danger either when operating normally or during a malfunction (such as failure of a thermostat that controls the operating temperature or during operation of a safety device). The safety requirements are shown in a logic diagram in Figure 13.

The general principle of G3 is that all hot water systems should have at least two independent levels of safety, in addition to thermostats used for normal control of water temperature.

This requirement applies to all hot water systems, not just the unvented systems that were covered by the previous edition of AD G (there have been two fatal incidents caused by failure of vented systems).

The safety of vented systems is achieved by a suitable vent pipe of not less than 19mm internal diameter, running from the top of the hot water storage vessel to a point over the cold water storage cistern that is open to the atmosphere and above water level and either:

a.   a device, in addition to any operational control thermostat, that prevents the temperature of the stored water exceeding 100°C at

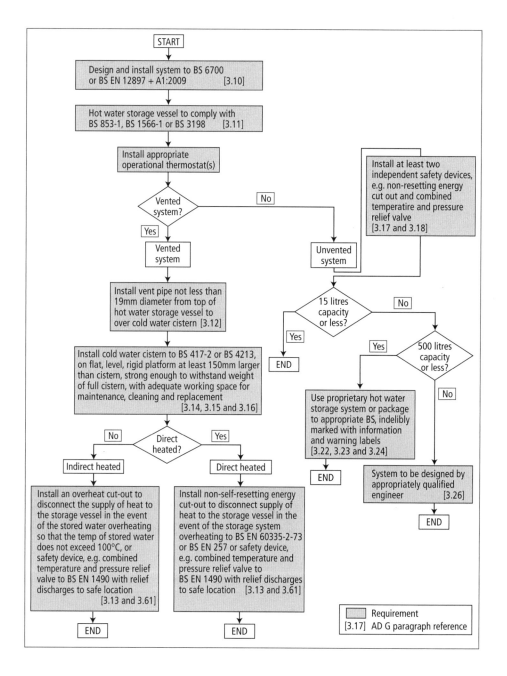

Figure 13
Logic diagram of safety hot water safety requirements

any time, fitted to either the heat source or the hot water storage vessel, either:

i. in the case of direct heat sources, a non-self-resetting energy cut-out to disconnect the supply of heat to the storage vessel in the event of the vessel overheating; and

ii. in the case of indirect heat sources, an overheat cut-out to disconnect the supply of heat to the storage vessel in the event of the stored water overheating so that the temperature of the stored water does not exceed 100°C; or

b. a temperature relief valve or a combined temperature and pressure relief valve, or some other safety device, to safely discharge the overheated water in to the atmosphere in locations where it will not endanger people in or around the building.

To prevent a recurrence of the circumstances that caused the death of two people in separate incidents, cisterns must be properly supported on a solid base designed to support the weight of a full cistern with an adequate factor of safety for maintenance and at least 150mm larger than the base of the cistern; they must not be supported directly on joists. This is illustrated in Figure 14. In addition, space must be provided above and around the cistern to enable proper maintenance, cleaning and replacement.

Proper support is particularly required for plastic cisterns, which should be in accordance with to BS 4213:2004. Metal cisterns should comply with BS 417-2:1987. Although metal cisterns are stronger and less affected by heat, and therefore inherently pose less of a risk of failure, they are more difficult to clean than a plastic cistern and need internal painting to prevent rusting; dirt and rust encourage the proliferation of *Legionella* bacteria.

Unvented systems have the potential to store huge quantities of energy, which if not properly controlled can lead to explosions. Safety is achieved in unvented systems by:

a.   at least two independent safety devices, in addition to any operational control thermostat, that prevent the temperature of the stored water exceeding 100°C at any time, fitted to the hot water storage vessel, or some other no less effective device; and

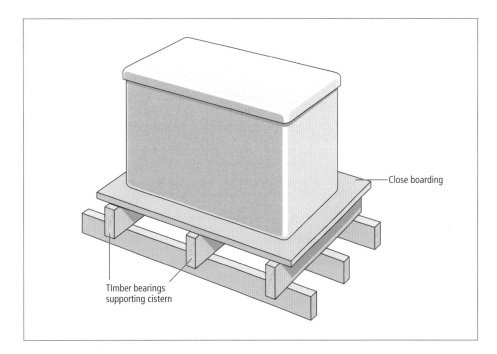

Close boarding

Timber bearings
supporting cistern

Figure 14
Support of cold water cistern. From the *Water Regulations Guide*, published by the Water Regulations Advisory Scheme Ltd

b.   discharging hot water from safety devices to the atmosphere in locations where they will not endanger people in or around the building.

3.4   Energy cut-outs and relief valves

An energy cut-out is a device that, during abnormal operation, limits the temperature of the controlled part by automatically opening the circuit, or by reducing the current, and is constructed so that its setting cannot be altered by the user. A non-self-resetting energy cut-out requires a manual operation for resetting, or replacement of a part, in order to restore the current. In a directly heated system the energy cut-out should be on the storage cylinder; in an indirect system, the sensor should be located on the storage cylinder, with the energy cut-out being fitted to the heating device.

In addition to the normal switching mechanism, electrical heaters must also include an independent non-self-resetting overtemperature cut-out safety device to prevent water in the hot water cylinder from overheating by complying with the relevant British Standard, as shown in Table 5.

Table 5
Electric water heating

Type of installation	Comply with
Immersion heater	BS EN 60335-2-73:2003
Instantaneous water heater	BS EN 60335-2-35:2002
Electric storage water heater	BS EN 60335-2-21:2003

Temperature relief valves are devices that open when the temperature reaches a predetermined temperature (95°C maximum) and discharge the overheated water to waste. They must comply with BS 6283-2 or -3 and be marked with the set temperature and the discharge rating. An air-break device is sometimes included to prevent implosion/collapse of the cylinder.

Combined temperature and pressure relief valves are devices that open when either the temperature or pressure reaches a predetermined value, in order to prevent the temperature of the water exceeding 100°C, and discharge the overheated water to waste. They must comply with BS EN 1490:2000.

To ensure that the temperature of the stored water does not exceed 100°C, temperature relief valves and combined temperature and pressure relief valves should be located directly on the storage vessel.

An in-line strainer should be installed to aid trouble-free function of relief valves.

3.5 Discharge pipes – layout, termination, size, traps, valves and marking

Discharges from relief valves should be routed from the hot water storage to a place that poses no risk to persons in the vicinity. A typical arrangement is illustrated in Figure 15.

Pipework should be:

- short pipe, D1, discharging to
- a tundish draining into
- discharge pipe, D2, that conveys overheated water to
- a safe termination point.

D1 should be:

- maximum 600mm long;

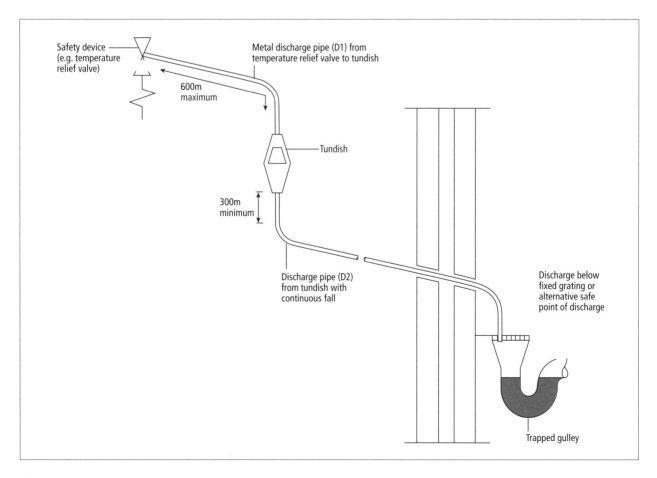

Figure 15
Typical arrangement of relief discharge pipework. © Crown copyright, 2009

- metal (the potential temperature rules out the use of plastics);
- have a diameter no smaller than the nominal size of the relief valve.

D1 pipes from several relief valves may be manifolded together, provided the manifold is sized to accept and discharge the total flow from all of the valves connected to it.

Tundishes should:

- be vertical;
- be located in the same space as the unvented hot water storage system;
- be fitted as close as possible to, and lower than, the relief valve;
- incorporate a suitable air gap;
- make any discharges visible (consideration should be given to a remote warning system in circumstances where the discharge may not be noticed).

Discharge pipe D2 should be:

- vertical for at least 300mm below the tundish;
- laid at a minimum gradient of 1:200;
- made of metal (or other material with demonstrated capability to safely withstand the temperatures, e.g. polybutylene (PB) or cross-linked polyethylene (PC-X) to Class S or BS 7291-2:2006, and marked to identify the product and performance standard);
- sized to Section D.2 of BS 6700:2006+A1:2009;
- (where more than one system connects into D2) one size larger than the largest individual pipe D2 connected to it.

Termination points should be in a safe place, such as:

- a trapped gully, with the end of pipe D2 below the fixed grating but above the water seal;
- about 100mm above an external surface, in a downward direction and through a wire cage or guard:
  - at low level;
  - at high level (e.g. into a metal hopper on a discharge pipe) with any discharge being visible and at least 3m away from any plastic guttering but not onto roofing or rainwater systems that would not be able to withstand the temperature of the discharge;
- into a soil stack, providing:
  - the stack is made from materials able to withstand the temperature of the discharge, e.g. metal;
  - sewer gas is prevented from escaping, without using a water seal (i.e. by using a mechanical seal, such as a Hepworth HepV0 valve);
  - D2 is installed as a separate pipe and continuously marked so that sanitary appliances are not connected to it.

BRE Information Paper 8/07 recommends that, if plastic is used for the discharge pipe between the mechanical valve and the stack, it should be polypropylene (PP) to BS EN 1451-1:2000. It also advises that the stack should be fully ventilated, i.e. without any gap or air admittance valve, and that PVCu stacks to BS EN 1329-1:2000 or BS 4514:2001 are suitable.

However, connection to a stack is recommended only for relief discharges from hot water storage vessels of 210 litres or less, and not for relief discharges from combi boilers or sealed system boilers.

3.6   Warning labels

Because unvented hot water storage systems (UHWSS) have the potential to contain extremely large amounts of energy, their safety relies upon the provision and maintenance of their safety devices.

In order to warn users that they have a UHWSS and to inform maintenance operators of where to seek spare parts or maintenance recommendations, a label as shown in Figure 16 should be fitted in a prominent position on the UHWSS.

The design of UHWSS larger than 500 litres capacity is likely to be bespoke. Therefore, in this case the standard label should not be used, as switching the unit off in the event of a flow from a discharge pipe may cause other problems. Instead, a warning label specified by the designer of the UHWSS should be displayed.

WARNING TO USER

a. Do not remove or adjust any component part of this unvented water heater; contact the installer.

b. If this unvented water heater develops a fault, such as a flow of hot water from the discharge pipe, switch the heater off and contact the installer.

WARNING TO INSTALLER

a. This installation is subject to the Building Regulations.

b. Use only appropriate components for installation or maintenance.

Installed by:

Name ....

Address ....

Tel. No. ....

Completion date ....

Figure 16
UHWSS warning label. © Crown copyright, 2009

3.7 Temperature limitation: domestic hot water distribution system

> The temperature of the domestic hot water distribution system should not exceed 60°C.

The Water Regulations state that water should be stored at not less than 60°C and distributed at a temperature of not less than 55°C (in order to prevent contamination of *Legionella* or similar pathogens), so the hot water should not be overcooled.

Several types of water heater, including solar heat collectors and solid fuel boilers, have no means of preventing the temperature of the water in the domestic hot water storage vessel from exceeding 80°C. (Water heated by gas or oil-fired boilers and electric immersion heaters tend to heat circulating water to lower temperatures.) To reduce the risk of scalding from hot pipework or hot water outlets that are not protected by a thermostatic mixing valve (TMV), the temperature in the domestic hot water distribution system should not exceed 60°C. This can be achieved by fitting a device at the outlet from the hot water storage vessel, such as an in-line hot water supply tempering valve in accordance with BS EN 15092 which introduces cold water.

3.8 Temperature limitation: delivered hot water

> The temperature of hot water delivered to baths should not exceed 48°C.

Each year, scalding baths are responsible for an average of 21 deaths and 615 serious injuries that can result in disfigurement for life. The very young and the very old, with thin skin, are the most vulnerable, with the elderly accounting for around 75% of the fatalities. People with a reduced ability to perceive risk or react to hazardous situations, such as those with mental or physical disabilities, are also at greater risk of injury.

The severity of scalding depends on:

- the temperature of the water;
- the volume of water;
- the sensitivity of the skin (young and elderly skin is particularly sensitive);

SCALDING EXAMPLES

A two-year-old boy falls into a bath of scalding hot water, sustaining massive burns to his body. By age of seven, he's experienced 100+ operations – 15 life-saving. He faces many more years of painful skin grafts until he stops growing. Requiring regular hospital treatment, he is sometimes confined to a wheelchair. His mother has been unable to undertake training opportunities or return to work. Projected cost of treating his injuries is £250,000.

(Reported on the Thermostatic Mixing Valves Manufacturers Association website)

Darren Fergusson, 17, from Stenhousemuir, suffered permanent facial disfigurement from scalding hot bath water when he was a baby. He has undergone 59 major operations, numerous minor operations and laser surgery since being scalded on the face and chest by bath water when he was just six months old. 'My physical injuries are plain for all to see. I have others which cannot be seen. I was robbed of my childhood, I had to grow up and face things that none of my friends had to face.'

(*Scotsman*, 25 November 2004)

The death of a woman who scalded herself at St Peter's Hospital in Chertsey was an accident, a coroner said. Shelaigh Robertson, 75, who lived locally and who was suffering from dementia, burned herself while having an unsupervised bath in July of this year. She later died at Chelsea and Westminster Hospital.

(BBC News website, 20 September 2002)

Holly Devonport from Wakefield was five years old when she suffered scalds to more than half her body. Her mother, Julie, was running a bath and went to get a fresh towel. Holly was perched on the edge of the bath, playing with her Gameboy, and in the split second when her mother left the room, she slipped and fell in. Her mother said that when she pulled Holly from the bath her legs looked like they had been dipped in acid. Holly's agonising injuries meant that she endured a seven-hour operation to graft skin from her stomach on to her legs. She spent six weeks in Pinderfields Hospital in Wakefield and six months in a wheelchair. She missed four months of school. She will be scarred for life.

(Hansard, 29 March 2006)

- the duration of exposure to hot water; in healthy adult skin, third-degree burns occur following exposure to
  - 46°C for five minutes
  - 55°C for 30 seconds
  - 60°C for five seconds
  - 70°C for less than one second.

A scald affecting more than one-fifth of the body has the same metabolic impact as being hit by a bus.

The risk of scalding is further increased if sensation or reaction time is reduced, as scalding may have already have occurred before the sensation of heat is recognised.

A comfortable temperature for a bath is around 38°C.

Although the regulation requires the water temperature to be limited only in baths, it is strongly recommended on safety grounds to consider limiting the temperature of water supplied to showers, bidets and basins. It should be noted that the temperature of 48°C for baths is a maximum and the design temperature should be lower; recommended temperatures for the maximum mixed hot water temperatures for safe use are given in Table 6.

Table 6
Recommended maximum mixed hot water temperature

Appliance	Temperature (°C)
Assisted bathing	46
Baths	44
Showers	41
Basins	41
Bidets	38

There is no recommended temperature limit on sinks because of the need for very hot water for washing up.

Limits on the water temperature of bidets, washbasins and shower were not included in the regulation because the total cost for England and Wales would outweigh the benefits, as scalding from basins and showers accounts for only 4% and 2.5% of scalding injuries respectively. However, the Scottish Building Standards require a temperature limit of 48°C at hot water supply outlets to bidets as well as baths, presumably because the taps on a bidet can be easily reached by a small child.

Hot water temperatures can be limited by fitting a thermostatic mixing valve (TMV). BuildCert operate two approval schemes for TMVs:

1. TMV2: for use in domestic properties, schools and hotels, based upon the requirements of BS EN 1111:1999 or BS EN 1287:1999.
2. TMV3: for use in healthcare facilities, nursing homes, young persons' care homes and schools for the severely disabled, based upon NHS Estates Model Engineering Specification D 08.

Under the TMV2 scheme, valves must:

- control temperature during normal operation;
- control temperature during cold water failure;
- be supplied with comprehensive instructions for installation and use;
- have appropriate requirements for maintenance;
- be compatible with the plumbing system.

For TMVs to function properly, they must be suitable for the hot and cold pressures and installed, commissioned and maintained in accordance with the manufacturer's instructions.

TMVs should be as close as possible to the outlet, to minimise the risk of colonisation by *Legionella* bacteria or other pathogens. Where outlets are used only occasionally, consideration should be given to making provisions for them to be flushed with high-temperature water.

Devices to limit the maximum temperature of hot water at outlets should not be easily alterable by building users.

3.9 Workmanship

Systems should be installed with good workmanship, in accordance with BS 8000-15.

3.10 Commissioning

Systems should be properly commissioned.

For hot water systems to be safe and work efficiently, they must be commissioned.

This may include:

- performance testing the system and controls to minimise energy consumption;
- calibration, setting and testing of automatic control systems.

Commissioning should be carried out in accordance with:

- for new and existing dwellings: the *Domestic Heating Compliance Guide* (see section 3.11);
- for buildings other than dwellings: Chartered Institute of Building Services Engineers (CIBSE) Commissioning Code M.

The Building Regulations (Regulation 20C(2) and the Building (Approved Inspectors, etc.) Regulations) require a notice of completion of commissioning to be given to the relevant building control body, within:

- five days of commissioning for work carried out under
    - a building notice
    - full plans
    - an initial notice
    - an amendment notice;
- 30 days of commissioning for work carried out by a competent person.

A completion/final certificate is unlikely to be given without receipt of a notice of completion of commissioning.

Records of commissioning should be included in the building health and safety file.

3.11 Relevant British Standards and other guidance

Reference	Publisher	Obtain and read?
BS 6700:2006+A1:2009 *Design, installation, testing and maintenance of services supplying water for domestic use within buildings and their curtilages*	BSI	Essential
Water Regulations Guide	Water Regulations Advisory Service (WRAS)	Essential
Water fittings and materials directory (www.wras.co.uk/Directory)	Water Regulations Advisory Service (WRAS)	Preferable Essential for detailed design and specification
BS EN 60335-2-73:2003 *Specification for safety of household and similar electrical appliances. Particular requirements. Fixed immersion heaters*	BSI	Unnecessary – but use in specification for electric immersion heaters
BS EN 60335-2-35:2002 *Specification for safety of household and similar electrical appliances*	BSI	Unnecessary – but use in specification for electric instantaneous heaters
BS EN 60335-2-21:2003 *Household and similar electrical appliances. Safety. Particular requirements for storage heaters*	BSI	Unnecessary – but use in specification for electric water storage heaters
BS EN 60730-2-9:2002 *Automatic electrical controls for household and similar use. Particular requirements for temperature sensing control*	BSI	Unnecessary – but use in specification for electric-fuelled hot water systems
BS EN 257:1992 *Mechanical thermostats for gas-burning appliances*	BSI	Unnecessary – but use in specification for gas-fuelled hot water systems
BS 6283-2:1991 *Safety and control devices for use in hot water systems. Specifications for temperature relief valves for pressures from 1 bar to 10 bar*	BSI	Unnecessary – but use in specifications of hot water systems
BS 6283-3:1991 *Safety and control devices for use in hot water systems. Specification for combined temperature and pressure relief valves for pressures from 1 bar to 10 bar*	BSI	Unnecessary – but use in specifications of hot water systems

Reference	Publisher	Obtain and read?
BS EN 1490:2000 *Building valves. Combined temperature and pressure relief valves. Tests and requirements*	BSI	Unnecessary – but use in specifications of hot water systems
BuildCert website for approved valves TMV2 and TMV3 (www.buildcert.com)	BuildCert	Unnecessary – but use in specifications of hot water systems
BS 417-2:1987 *Specification for galvanized low carbon steel cisterns, cistern lids, tanks and cylinders. Metric units*	BSI	Unnecessary – but use in specifications of hot water systems
BS 4213:2004 *Cisterns for domestic use. Cold water storage and combined feed and expansion (thermoplastic) cisterns up to 500 litres. Specification*	BSI	Unnecessary – but use in specifications of hot water systems
BS 853-1:1996 *Specification for vessels for use in heating systems. Calorifiers and storage vessels for central heating and hot water supply*	BSI	Unnecessary – but use in specifications of hot water systems
BS 1566-1:2002 *Copper indirect cylinders for domestic purposes. Open vented copper cylinders. Requirements and test methods*	BSI	Unnecessary – but use in specifications of hot water systems
BS 3198:1981 *Specification for copper hot water storage combination units for domestic purposes*	BSI	Unnecessary – but use in specifications of hot water systems
BS 8000-15:1990 *Workmanship on building sites. Code of practice for hot and cold water services (domestic scale)*	BSI	Unnecessary – but use in specifications Essential for installation and site supervision
Domestic Heating Compliance Guide: compliance with Approved Documents: L1A: New dwellings and L1B: Existing dwellings, 2nd edition, December 2008	CLG	Unecessary but use in specifications
CIBSE Commissioning Code M: Commissioning management	CIBSE	Unnecessary – but use in specifications Essential for commissioning and site supervision
BS 5918:1989 *Code of practice for solar heating systems for domestic hot water*	BSI	Essential for design of solar heating systems
prCEN/TS 12977-1:2008 *Thermal solar systems and components. Custom built systems. General requirement*	BSI	Essential for design of solar heating systems

Reference	Publisher	Obtain and read?
BS EN 15092:2008 *Building valves. In line hot water supply tempering valves. Tests and requirements*	BSI	Unnecessary – but use in specifications
Information Paper 8/07 Self-sealing waste valves for domestic use: An assessment	BRE	Useful for discharge of relief valves to stacks

Sanitary conveniences and washing facilities (G4)

4.1   The requirement

> **SANITARY CONVENIENCES AND WASHING FACILITIES**
>
> **G4**
> (1)   Adequate and suitable sanitary conveniences must be provided in rooms provided to accommodate them or in bathrooms.
> (2)   Adequate hand washing facilities must be provided in:
>   (a)   rooms containing sanitary conveniences; or
>   (b)   rooms or spaces adjacent to rooms containing sanitary conveniences.
> (3)   Any room containing a sanitary convenience, a bidet or any facility for washing hands provided in accordance with paragraph (2)(b) must be separated from any kitchen or any area where food is prepared.
>
> **Limits on application**
> None.

4.2   How does this fit in with Water Regulations, Workplace Regulations and other Parts of the Building Regulations?

The provision of sanitary facilities in buildings is covered by numerous different regulations. Table 7 identifies the main regulations, standards and guidance documents affecting the design and provision of sanitary accommodation for most applications. It should be noted that more rigorous requirements apply to special types of buildings, such as schools and hospitals. Certain providers (such as railways and airport operators) also have their own standards, which should not be lower than the legal requirements.

Table 7
Other regulations associated with sanitary conveniences and washing facilities

Associated area	Regulation	Specifications/guides
Workplaces	Workplace (Health, Safety and Welfare) Regulations 1992 As amended by: • Quarries Miscellaneous Health and Safety Provisions Regulations 1995 • Quarries Regulations 1999 • Health and Safety (Miscellaneous Amendments) Regulations 2002 • Work at Height Regulations 2005 • Construction (Design and Management) Regulations 2007	*Workplace Health, Safety and Welfare. Workplace (Health, Safety and Welfare) Regulations 1992. Approved Code of Practice*, L24. HSE Books 1998*. BS 6465-1:2006+A1:2009 *Sanitary installations. Code of practice for the design of sanitary facilities and scales of provision of sanitary and associated applicances* BS 6465-2:1996 *Sanitary installations. Code of practice for space requirements for sanitary appliances* BS 6465-3:2006 *Sanitary installations. Code of practice for the selection, installation and maintenance of sanitary and associated appliances*
Water	Water Supply (Water Fittings) Regulations 1999	*Water Regulations Guide* BS 6700:2006+A1:2009 *Design, installation, testing and maintenance of services supplying water for domestic use within buildings and their curtilages*
Electricity	IEE Wiring Regulations 17th Edition	BS 7671:2008 *Requirements for electrical installations*
	Building Regulations 2000 Schedule 1 Part P (Electrical safety – Dwellings)	Approved Document P
Ventilation	Building Regulations 2000 Schedule 1 Part F (Ventilation)	Approved Document F
Disabled access	Building Regulations 2000 Schedule 1 (as amended by SI 2003/2692) Part M	Approved Document M, Access to and Use of Buildings BS 8300:2009 *Design of buildings and their approaches to meet the needs of disabled people. Code of practice*

*The regulations contained in this Approved Code of Practice have been amended by the Quarries Regulations 1999, the Health and Safety (Miscellaneous Amendments) Regulations 2002, the Work at Height Regulations 2005 and the Construction (Design and Management) Regulations 2007

The principal piece of legislation covering the provision of sanitary conveniences is the Workplace (Health, Safety and Welfare) Regulations 1992. Other legislation, including Part G, aligns with at least the minimum provision of these regulations. They cover a wide range of basic health, safety and welfare issues and apply to most workplaces (with the exception of those workplaces involving work on construction sites, those in or on a ship, or those below ground at a mine). They are amended by the Quarries Regulations 1999, the Health and Safety (Miscellaneous Amendments) Regulations 2002, the Work at Height Regulations 2005 and the Construction (Design and Management) Regulations 2007.

Employers have a general duty under Section 2 of the Health and Safety at Work etc. Act 1974 to ensure, so far as is reasonably practicable, the health, safety and welfare of their employees at work. People in control of non-domestic premises have a duty (under Section 4 of the Act) towards people who are not their employees but use their premises. The regulations expand on these duties and are intended to protect the health and safety of everyone in the workplace, and to ensure that adequate welfare facilities are provided for people at work.

The Workplace (Health, Safety and Welfare) Regulations 1992 apply to a wide range of workplaces in addition to factories, shops and offices, including, for example, schools, hospitals, hotels and places of entertainment. The term 'workplace' also includes the common parts of shared buildings, private roads and paths on industrial estates and business parks, and temporary work sites (except workplaces involving construction work on construction sites).

The regulations do not apply to domestic premises (i.e. private dwellings), and exclude homeworkers. However, they do apply to hotels, nursing homes and to parts of workplaces where 'domestic' staff are employed, such as hostel kitchens.

The Workplace (Health, Safety and Welfare) Regulations also require the sanitary facilities to be kept clean and properly maintained. Surfaces in rooms containing sanitary conveniences should be cleanable, but there are no specific requirements for cleaners' sinks (although BS 6465-1:2006+A1:2009 gives recommendations for the design and scale of provision of cleaners' rooms).

Sanitary conveniences and washing facilities are covered by Regulations 20 and 21 respectively. Suitable and sufficient sanitary conveniences and washing facilities should be provided in readily accessible places. They and the rooms containing them should be kept clean and be adequately ventilated and lit. Washing facilities should have running hot and cold or warm water, soap and clean towels or other means of cleaning or drying.

If required by the type of work, showers should also be provided. Men and women should have separate facilities unless each facility is in a separate room with a lockable door and is for use by only one person at a time.

The regulations aim to ensure that workplaces meet the health, safety and welfare needs of all members of a workforce, including people with disabilities.

The Disability Discrimination Act 1995 does not lay down any standards but does require employers and those who provide a service to the public (banks, shops, theatres, etc.) to make any 'reasonable' adjustments to their premises necessary to enable disabled people to use the service. Compliance with Part M of the Building Regulations is accepted as satisfying the requirements of this act in new buildings. Ideally, existing premises should also comply with the requirements of Part M, but the size of the premises and the financial status of the occupier will also be relevant in deciding what is reasonable. Part M also covers additional design features such as the height of urinals and washbasins. BS 8300:2009 *Design of buildings and their approaches to meet the needs of disabled people. Code of practice* provides additional information to that given in Part M, particularly in respect of fixtures and fittings.

The Workplace (Health, Safety and Welfare) Regulations give the minimum numbers of sanitary appliances (referred to as the 'scale of provision') for both men and women. The HSE Approved Code of Practice L24 provides guidance.

Care should be taken in assessing the scale of provision in order to ensure that there is not underprovision for women (i.e. women would have to queue for toilets), as this would be contrary to the Equality Act 2006. The scale of provision for women given in BS 6465-1:2006+A1:2009 is higher than in the HSE Approved Code of Practice. The use of BS 6465-1:2006+A1:2009 will help to avoid discrimination, as this provides equal numbers of sanitary conveniences for men and women. However, research shows that women take about twice as long as men in using sanitary conveniences, and it could be argued that their provision should be higher than that for men, not just equal.

The Food Standards Agency's Code of Practice, *Food Hygiene – a Guide for Business,* gives advice on complying with the Food Hygiene Regulations.[1] It emphasises the need for effective hand washing to help prevent harmful bacteria from spreading from people's hands to food, work surfaces, equipment, etc. To enable staff to wash their hands properly, there must be an adequate number of washbasins, suitably located and used only for cleaning hands, supplied with wholesome hot and cold running water and materials for cleaning hands and for hygienic drying. The Code of Practice also states that there must be an adequate number of flush lavatories, connected to an effective drainage system, and that toilets must not open directly into rooms where food is handled.

> Parts 1, 2 and 3 of BS 6465 *Sanitary installations* provides comprehensive guidance for sanitary facilities in buildings. They are compatible with the various other regulations and are updated regularly to maintain compatibility. BS 6465 may be used as an alternative to Approved Document G to demonstrate compliance with requirement G4 and can therefore be regarded as a reliable source of information for all projects.

The Local Government (Miscellaneous Provisions) Act 1976 allows local authorities to require adequate sanitary provision in various types of premises.

BS 6465-3:2006 *Sanitary installations. Code of practice for the selection, installation and maintenance of sanitary and associated appliances* gives recommendations on the selection and installation of appliances. Consideration should be given to the water efficiency of appliances, as well as ensuring that they meet the requirements of the Water Regulations.

4.3   Scale of provision in dwellings

> Any dwelling (house or flat) must have at least one WC and associated hand washing facility. It should comply with Approved Document M and therefore should be on the principal/entrance storey of the dwelling.
>
> Where additional WCs and urinals are provided, each should have an associated hand washing facility.

Table 8 gives guidance on how many sanitary appliances in excess of the minimum should be provided, but reference should be made to BS 6465-1:2006+A1:2009 for additional recommendations.

Table 8
Minimum provision of sanitary appliances for private dwellings

Type of sanitary appliance	Number to be provided per dwelling
WC	1 for up to four people; 2 for five people or more
Washbasin (in or adjacent to every toilet)	1
Bath or shower (requirement G5)	1 per four people
Kitchen sink (requirement G6)	1

4.4 Scale of provision in buildings other than dwellings – how many toilets should a workplace have?

Enough sanitary conveniences must be provided appropriate for the sex and age of building users.

BS 6465-1:2006+A1:2009 *Sanitary installations. Code of practice for the design of sanitary facilities and scales of provision of sanitary and associated appliances* provides comprehensive guidance for sanitary facilities in buildings other than and including dwellings.

Approved document M gives the minimum sanitary accommodation to be provided to meet the likely needs of disabled people, which may form part of the total provision.

Tables 9 to 11 give the minimum requirements recommended in BS 6465-1:2006+A1:2009 for sanitary appliances for typical situations, but reference should be made to BS 6465-1 for additional guidance. These numbers are larger than those given in the HSE Approved Code of Practice L24, in order to make equal provision for men and women.

If the number of occupants in an office is not known at the design stage, BS 6465-1:2006+A1:2009 recommends designing the toilet provision for 120% of the population (60% male, 60% female) based on one person per 12m² of usable floor space for normal offices. Where unisex toilets are provided provision may be based upon 100% of the population. Consideration should be given to change to high-density use, such as call centres, which may be based upon one person per 6m² of usable floor space.

Table 9
Minimum provision of sanitary appliances for staff toilets in offices, shops, factories and similar workplaces (for female staff and male staff where urinals not installed)

Number of people at work	Number of WCs and washbasins
1 to 5	1
6 to 15	2
16 to 30	3
31 to 45	4
46 to 60	5
61 to 75	6
76 to 90	7
91 to 100	8
More than 100	8 plus one WC and washbasin for each 25 people (rounded up)

Table 10
Minimum provision of sanitary appliances for staff toilets in offices, shops, factories and similar workplaces (for male staff only where urinals installed)

Number of people at work	Number of WCs and washbasins	Number of urinals
1 to 15	1	1
16 to 30	2	1
31 to 45	2	2
46 to 60	3	2
61 to 75	3	3
76 to 90	4	3
91 to 100	4	4
More than 100	4 plus one WC, urinal and washbasin for each 50 males (rounded up)	

Table 11
Minimum provision of sanitary appliances for bedrooms in hotels, hostels and similar accommodation

Type of accommodation	Type of sanitary appliance	Number to be provided per dwelling
Bedrooms with en-suite accommodation	WC, washbasin and either bath or shower	1 per bedroom
Bedrooms without en-suite accommodation	WC	1 per nine people
	Washbasin	1 per bedroom; 1 per four people in dormitories
	Bathroom (containing bath or shower, washbasin and additional WC	1 per four people

4.5 Layout of facilities

BS 6465-2:1996 *Sanitary installations. Code of practice for space requirements for sanitary appliances* gives recommendations for the different areas needed for sanitary fittings, as shown in Table 12.

Table 12
Areas associated with sanitary appliances

Name of area	Description
Appliance space	Area needed for the sanitary appliance and, where applicable, any closely related pipework and fittings
Activity space	Area needed for the user to carry out the activity normally associated with the appliance and to enable cleaning and routine maintenance to be carried out
Circulation space	Obstruction-free area for access to an appliance without interference to users of other appliances
Luggage zone	Area needed for temporary storage of personal belongings within a WC cubicle. This space may also be used for the temporary parking of pushchairs, prams or shopping trolleys. The actual dimensions of the area should be appropriate to the type of luggage that would normally be expected at that facility

As well as the sanitary appliances and areas needed to use them, space should also be included for some or all of the following:

- toilet roll holders;
- towels or hand dryers (remember that it generally takes longer to dry hands using an electric dryer than to wash them);
- chair or stool;
- laundry basket;
- waste bin;
- sanitary towel disposal bin;
- shelf to accommodate washing accessories (windows sill may provide this if low enough);
- mirror;
- electric shaver point;
- lockable medicine cupboard.

Hand washing facilities must be provided in, or adjacent to, rooms containing sanitary conveniences (i.e. WCs and urinals) and should be sited, designed and installed so as not to be prejudicial to health.

Sanitary accommodation should be arranged with a washbasin between the WC and door, to encourage hand washing.

Rooms containing sanitary conveniences (i.e. WCs and urinals) and/or hand washing facilities should be separated from a place used for food preparation by a door, as shown in Figures 17 and 18.

Hand washing facilities should be located either in the room containing the sanitary conveniences (i.e. WCs and urinals) or in an adjacent room that provides the sole means of access to the sanitary conveniences (provided that it is not used for the preparation of food).

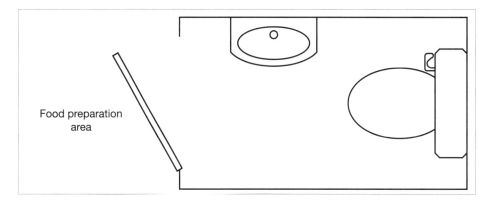

Figure 17
Separation between hand washbasin/WC and food preparation area – single room. © Crown copyright, 2009

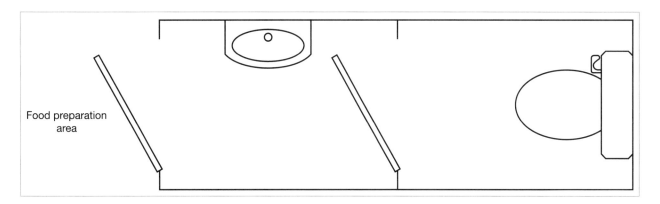

Figure 18
Separation between hand washbasin/WC and food preparation area – two rooms. © Crown copyright, 2009

Different ways of arranging sanitary conveniences (i.e. WCs and urinals) in non-domestic dwellings are illustrated in Figure 19.

Although a self-contained room has the advantages of privacy and flexibility (it can be designated for the use of males, females or both), users tend to occupy the room for a longer time, during which the appliances are unavailable to other users; thus, the effective provision is reduced. To overcome this, the WC provision should be increased by 25%.

Although BS 6465-1:2006+A1:2009 recommends one hot-air dryer for three washbasins (or one towel for four washbasins), there is often a hold-up because it takes longer to dry hands than to wash them, Therefore, consideration should be given to providing more than the recommended minimum.

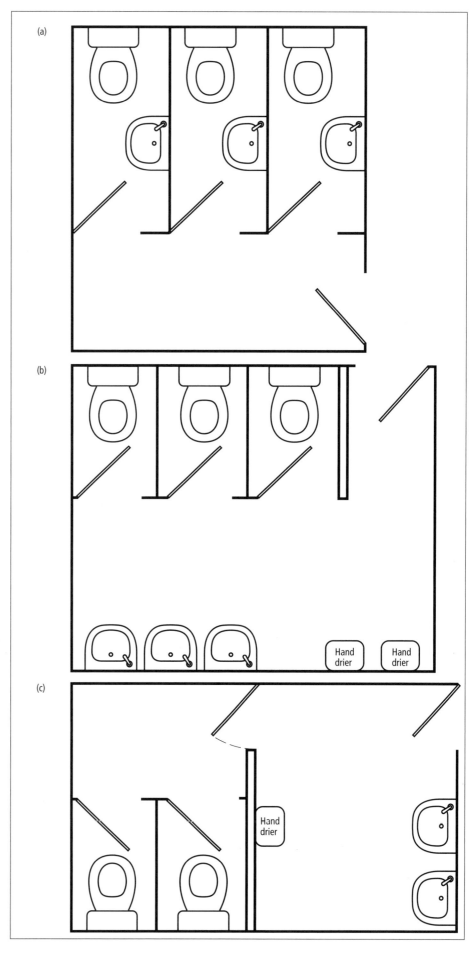

Figure 19
Typical sanitary convenience arrangements. (a) A self-contained room which also contains hand washing facilities. (b) A room with shared hand washing facilities containing a number of cubicles. (c.) A self-contained room with hand-washing facilities in adjacent room

4.6   Waterless appliances

4.6.1   Waterless toilets

WCs that are not flushed with water and discharged to a sewerage system comprise:

- drying toilets;
- chemical toilets;
- composting toilets.

Drying toilets use electricity (or some other form of energy) to dry the contents of the WC; the resulting dried material is then composted. However, Approved Document G specifically requires that energy should be used only for ventilation or sustaining the composting process, which therefore rules out this type of toilet.

Chemical toilets are most commonly found on aeroplanes and trains and in caravans and motorhomes or other places which do not have a sewerage system (e.g. construction sites and at outdoor gatherings such as music festivals). Portable toilets are universally chemical toilets. Chemical toilets store the waste until it can be conveniently emptied into a sewerage system and use chemicals to deodorise and break it down (for ease of emptying).

Composting toilets (also called biological, dry or waterless toilets) are systems that treat human excrement through biological processes, turning it into organic compost material that can be used to fertilise the soil. They are small-scale, complete sewage processing systems not connected to a water supply or a sewerage system.

The use of composting toilets was once confined to locations that did not have an adequate supply of water or sewage treatment system. Nowadays, they are increasingly being viewed as being more sustainable than traditional WCs by providing the following environmental benefits:

- water use is reduced;
- they do not contribute to sewer flows (reducing the risk of overflows) and effluent discharges;
- they provide compost;
- no energy is needed (except for units that use electric fans for ventilation);
- they have less potential to pollute sensitive groundwater than the alternatives of discharging septic tank effluent or effluent from a package sewage treatment plant into the ground.

TYPES OF COMPOSTING TOILETS

There are many different types of composting toilets, ranging from simple DIY designs to advanced high-tech proprietary models. They can be classified as:

- Self-contained: the composting container is housed in the toilet.
- Remote: the toilet is located separately from the composting site.
- Batch: waste is collected and composted in two or more sealed containers, mounted on a rotating carousel. When one container is full it is replaced with an empty one.
- Continual process: waste is composted in a single container, with compost being harvested from the bottom at regular intervals.

 OPERATION OF COMPOSTING TOILETS

Composting toilets decompose waste by creating aerobic conditions for bacteria, fungi, worms and other macro- and micro-organisms to thrive. The objective is to destroy harmful pathogens, reducing the risk to human health and the environment, and transform the waste nutrients into fertile soil. Waste is generally broken down to around 10% of the original volume over a period of two years or so.

Compost that is too wet becomes anaerobic and produces unpleasant smells. To avoid this problem, some composting toilets separate the urine from the faeces, either by the design of the toilet bowl or by a drain in the composting zone. The collected urine is high in nitrogen, potassium and phosphorus, so it is ideal for use as a fertiliser (on non-food plants) in water or infiltrated into the ground. Other models collect urine and faeces together, and either evaporate the liquid completely or require the addition of carbon material (referred to as a 'soak'), such as sawdust, leaf mould, straw or grass clippings, to soak up the liquid.

To prevent odours, the composting chamber generally requires ventilation to the air outside, either using a fan or by natural ventilation. This ventilation helps to evaporate liquid and increases the air supply needed for the aerobic digestion process. It also tends to create a negative pressure inside the toilet, resulting air in the room being replaced by fresh air.

The speed of decomposition can be speeded up by heating, either by using energy or by solar design.

Many systems require space, preferably with more than one composting chamber that can be accessed from outside the building to facilitate inspection and emptying. However, there are compact models available that contain the sewage inside a compost zone integral with the toilet pedestal, which is emptied as necessary to a separate external composting area.

Chemical and composting toilets may be used only where:

a.   suitable arrangements can be made for the disposal of the waste either on- or off-site; and

b.   the waste can be removed from the premises without carrying it through any living space or food preparation area (including a kitchen); and

c.   no part of the installation would be located in any places where it might be rendered ineffective by the entry of flood water.

Currently, there are no British or European standards for composting toilets.

4.6.2   Waterless urinals

Waterless urinals are similar to normal urinals except that they are not flushed with water. Advantages of waterless urinals include:

- water savings;
- reduced incidence of blockages (limescale is precipitated by the reaction of urine upon the flushing water; if the limescale is not removed, it will become colonised by bacteria that cause odour problems);
- no need for cisterns, flush pipes and flush controllers;
- no floods to cause damage.

However, it is essential that simple routine maintenance is carried out to keep them functioning properly.

TYPES OF WATERLESS URINALS

- Barrier systems, where urine and debris pass through a trap that has a layer of oil floating on top, to prevent odour. In some systems, the barrier fluid is contained within a cartridge that also intercepts hair and debris, which is replaced roughly two to six times a year, depending upon the amount of use.
- Microbiological systems, where micro-organisms are dosed from a block in the dome of the urinal outlet into the urinal trap to break down the urine. This is intended to prevent the build-up of urine sludge and deter the build-up of other bacteria that cause odours.
- Trap systems, where urine passes through a one-way plastic valve to prevent air from escaping from the sanitary pipework back into the building.

Drainage must comply with the requirements of Approved Document H1.

A conventional flushed WC should discharge to an adequate system of drainage. A water-flushed urinal should discharge to an adequate system of drainage by way of:

- a grating (to retain solid matter which could otherwise lead to blockages of the drainage system and increase the loading on sewage treatment plants);
- a trap or mechanical seal (to prevent foul gas coming from the drains);
- fixed pipework.

Macerating and pumping units must comply with BS EN 12050-1:2001 or BS EN 12050-3:2001 and may be used only if there is an alternative sanitary facility discharging directly to a gravity system.

Where it is not practicable to connect a WC (with or without other sanitary appliances used for personal washing) directly to a drainage system operated by gravity, AD G permits them to be connected to a packaged pumping plant that macerates (i.e. shreds) any solids before pumping the flow to a gravity system through small-bore pipework. In order to obtain reasonable performance, AD G states that units should either incorporate a macerator or use larger pumps and pipework and be specified to:

- BS EN 12050-1:2001 *Wastewater lifting plants for buildings and sites. Principles of construction and testing. Lifting plants for wastewater containing faecal matter*; or
- where the number of users is small and the plant serves no more than a single WC to which it is directly connected, one washbasin, one shower and one bidet located in the same room as the WC, to BS EN 12050-3:2001 *Wastewater lifting plants for buildings and sites. Principles of construction and testing. Lifting plants for wastewater containing faecal matter for limited applications.*

In the event of a failure of a macerator or pump (e.g. as a result of blockage or failure of controls or power), users must be able to use another sanitary appliance which does not rely on pumping in order to ensure a continued access to sanitary accommodation.

4.6.3   Reduced flows in drainage systems

One potential drawback of using less water is increased problems in drains and sewers.

Solids in drain and sewer systems, particularly at the upstream end, tend to be moved in a series of steps, with each discharge moving the solid further forwards. Long-duration flows, such as those from baths, are particularly helpful in moving solids and keeping the system self-cleansing. If the volume of flows is reduced, the self-cleansing action in drains becomes less effective. However, Report SR632 by HR Wallingford indicates that, if traditional gradients as shown in Table 13 are used (or steeper if possible), the reduction in self-cleansing action should not cause practical problems unless greywater recycling is used; this is contradicted by WRc Report CP367. Until clear industry-wide agreement is obtained, WCs with a minimum main flush volume of 4.5 litres are recommended.

Table 13
Self-cleansing gradients

Pipe size (diameter nominal, DN)	Gradient (1 in …)
100	40
150	60
225	90

Greywater recycling will result in few long-duration flows occurring (e.g. during overflow of the greywater system) and therefore makes drain cleaning more likely to be needed.

With all reduced flows, the risk of blockage will increase, so it is more important than ever that inappropriate items, such as nappies, are disposed with solid waste and not into the drainage system, i.e. 'bag it and bin it'.

If a drainage system is to be designed for very low flows, it is worthwhile considering the introduction of flushing syphons in the system (i.e. a vessel or chamber that will fill up; once full, syphonic action will empty it to produce a long-duration flush). Care will need to be taken in the design of such a chamber to avoid the contents becoming septic and causing odour problems. Proprietary units are available that can be installed on stacks and in chambers.

4.7   Relevant British Standards and other guidance

Reference	Publisher	Obtain and read?
BS 6465-1:2006+A1:2009 *Sanitary Installations. Code of practice for the design of sanitary facilities and scales of provision of sanitary and associated appliances*	BSI	Essential for buildings other than houses
BS 6465-2:1996 *Sanitary installations. Code of practice for space requirements for sanitary appliances*	BSI	Essential for layout
BS 6465-3:2006 *Sanitary installations. Code of practice for the selection, installation and maintenance of sanitary and associated appliances*	BSI	Optional
Workplace (Health, Safety and Welfare) Regulations 1992 (as amended by the Quarries Miscellaneous Health and Safety Provisions Regulations 1995). Approved code of practice and guidance (Health and Safety: Legal Series L 24)	Health and Safety Executive	Essential to determine minimum numbers of toilets in workplaces (fewer than BS 6465-1:2006+A1:2009)
Water Fittings and Materials Directory	Water Regulations Advisory Scheme	Essential for checking that fitting and materials comply with the Water Regulations
Water Regulations Guide	WRc	Essential for detailed design and installation of water supply systems

Reference	Publisher	Obtain and read?
Good Loo Design Guide (2004 edition)	RIBA Enterprises	Useful design data, particularly for the design for the disabled
BS 8300:2009 *Design of buildings and their approaches to meet the needs of disabled people – Code of practice*	BSI	Essential for the design of buildings other than single dwellings
Metric Handbook – Planning And Design Data, 3rd Edition. Part 5 – *Design basics: buildings and movement*	ArcPress 2007	Useful design data
Lauchlan CS, Escarameia M and Kellagher RBB. *Implications for Site Drainage Design of Low Water Usage in Domestic Buildings.* HR Report SR 632	HR Wallingford 2003	Optional – background reading
Pull the chain, fill the drain. CP367 – The effect of reduced water usage on sewer solid movement in small pieces	WRc	Optional – background reading

Note

1. The Food Hygiene (England) Regulations 2006 (SI 2006/14) and The Food Hygiene (Wales) Regulations 2006 (SI 2006/31 W.5).

Bathrooms (G5)

5.1 The requirement

 BATHROOMS

G5
A bathroom must be provided containing a washbasin and either a fixed bath or shower.

Limits on application
Requirement G5 applies only in dwellings and to buildings containing one or more rooms for residential purposes.

Requirement G5 applies to dwellings and buildings containing a room or rooms for residential purposes, such as hostels and halls of residence. A 'room for residential purposes' is defined in AD G as:

> a room, or a suite of rooms, which is not a dwelling-house or a flat and which is used by one or more persons to live and sleep in, and includes a room in a hostel, a hotel, a boarding house, a hall of residence or a residential home, whether or not the room is separated from or arranged in a cluster group with other rooms, but does not include a room in a hospital, or other similar establishment, used for patient accommodation and, for the purposes of this definition, a 'cluster' is a group of rooms for residential purposes which is (a) separate from the rest of the building in which it is situated by a door which is designed to be locked; and (b) not designed to be occupied by a single household.

Therefore, G5 does not apply to offices, factories, shops, etc. that do not have a room for residential purposes.

Bathrooms must also comply with various other regulations, specifications and guidance, as shown in Table 14.

Table 14
Other regulations associated with bathrooms

Associated area	Regulation	Specifications/guides
Scale of provision and spatial requirements		BS 6465-1:2006+A1:2009 *Sanitary installations. Code of practice for the design of sanitary facilities and scales of provision of sanitary and associated appliances*
		BS 6465-2:1996 *Sanitary installations. Code of practice for space requirements for sanitary appliances*
		BS 6465-3:2006 *Sanitary installations. Code of practice for the selection, installation and maintenance of sanitary and associated appliances*
Water	Water Supply (Water Fittings) Regulations 1999	*Water Regulations Guide*
		BS 6700:2006+A1:2009 *Specification for design, installation, testing and maintenance of services supplying water for domestic use within buildings and their curtilages*
Electricity	IEE Wiring Regulations 17th Edition	BS 7671:2008 *Requirements for electrical installations*
	Building Regulations 2000 Schedule 1 Part P (Electrical safety – Dwellings)	Approved Document P
Ventilation	Building Regulations 2000 Schedule 1 Part F (Ventilation)	Approved Document F
Drainage	Building Regulations 2000 Schedule 1 Part H (Drainage and waste disposal)	Approved Document H1 Sanitary pipework
		BS EN 12056:2 *Drainage inside buildings*

Where hot and cold taps are provided on a sanitary appliance, the hot tap should be on the left.

To reduce the risk of scalding and wastage of water associated with the wrong tap being opened, where hot and cold taps are provided on a sanitary appliance or sink, the hot tap should be on the left.

5.2 Bath or shower?

Showers have benefits and disadvantages in terms of water and energy use when compared with baths, as shown in Table 15.

Table 15
Comparison of showers and baths

Feature	Showers	Baths
Space	Can be installed in a small space (typically 1.6m² or more including activity space)	More space needed (typically 2.6m² or more including activity space)
Time	Quicker. Showering typically takes around four minutes. Drying time same as bath	Slower. Bathing typically takes 15 minutes. Drying time same as shower
Multiperson use	Because it is quicker and requires less cleaning than a bath, showers are more suitable for multiperson use	Bath water can be shared
Children	Difficulties with reaching controls, danger of slips and falls. Unsuitable for babies	Reduced depths and temperatures can be used Easier supervision Probably more enjoyable
Elderly and infirm	Level access preferable Danger of slips and trips, particularly where there is a step Easier for disabled to sit under shower	Easier supervision Difficulty in exiting but specialist baths and devices are available to reduce problems
Water supply system	For good showering, reasonable pressure needed Except for power showers, less water needed, typically 6–10l/min, using 24–60 litres per four-minute shower	For reasonable fill time, flow needed in order of 18l/min per tap; pressure less important Except where baths water is shared, more water used, typically 90 litres for a standard bath
Floor and wall construction	Walls need to be proofed against water ingress Mould is a potential problem on surfaces of cubicles and curtains	Floors need to be proofed against water overspilling
Availability	Freely available in different styles (e.g. trays, *in situ*, wet rooms) Specialist showers available (e.g. side sprays)	Freely available in many styles and colours Specialist baths available (e.g. whirlpool, spas, space-saving, side entry)
Other	Usually considered to be invigorating	Usually considered to be relaxing With a suitable curtain or screen, baths can be used for both showering and bathing

5.3   Scale of provision

BS 6465-1:2006+A1:2009 *Sanitary Installations. Code of practice for the design of sanitary facilities and scales of provision of sanitary and associated appliances* provides comprehensive guidance for sanitary facilities in dwellings, as well as for other buildings.

Table 16 shows the BS 6465-1:2006+A1:2009 recommendations on how many sanitary appliances in excess of the minimum should be provided per dwelling but reference should be made to BS 6465-1 for additional recommendations.

Table 17 shows the BS 6465-1:2006+A1:2009 recommendations on how many sanitary appliances in excess of the minimum should be provided in buildings other than dwellings with rooms for residential purposes. Again, reference should be made to BS 6465-1 for additional guidance.

Table 16
Minimum provision of sanitary appliances for private dwellings

Type of sanitary appliance	Number to be provided per dwelling
WC (requirement G4)	1 for up to four people; 2 for five people or more
Washbasin (in or adjacent to every toilet)	1
Bath or shower	1 per four people
Kitchen sink (requirement G6)	1

Table 17
Minimum provision of sanitary appliances for bedrooms in hotels, hostels and similar accommodation

Type of accommodation	Type of sanitary appliance	Number to be provided per dwelling
Bedrooms with en-suite accommodation	WC, washbasin and either bath or shower	1 per bedroom
Bedrooms without en-suite accommodation	WC	1 per nine people
	Washbasin	1 per bedroom; 1 per four people in dormitories
	Bathroom (containing bath or shower, washbasin and additional WC)	1 per four people

5.4 Layout of facilities

BS 6465-2:1996 *Sanitary installations. Code of practice for space requirements for sanitary appliances* gives recommendations for the different areas needed for sanitary fittings.

Approved Document M gives additional requirements for sanitary accommodation that take into account the needs of disabled people.

As well as the sanitary appliances and areas needed to use them, space should also be included for some or all of the following:

- toilet roll holders;
- towels;
- chair or stool;
- laundry basket;
- waste bin;
- shelf to accommodate washing accessories, (windows sill may provide this if low enough);
- mirror;
- electric shaver point;
- lockable medicine cupboard.

There is a huge number of ways in which bathrooms can be arranged, and Figure 20 illustrates a typical layout, indicating appliance and activity spaces. In the figure, activity spaces overlap and it would be preferable to have a larger room or to use space-saving appliances.

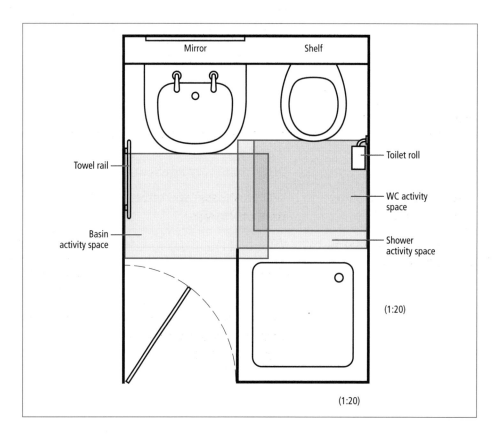

Figure 20
Typical shower room, with adequate space

5.5   Pumped discharges to drain

> Macerating and pumping units must comply with BS EN 12050-2:2001 and may be used only if there is an alternative sanitary facility discharging directly to a gravity system.

Where it is not practicable to connect sanitary appliances used for personal washing directly to a drainage system operated by gravity, AD G permits them to be connected to a packaged pumping plant that pumps the flow to a gravity system through small-bore pipework. It should be noted that BS EN 12056:1 requires drainage by gravity wherever practicable.

In order to obtain reasonable performance, AD G states that packaged pumping plants should comply with BS EN 12050-2:2001 *Wastewater lifting plants for buildings and sites. Principles of construction and testing. Lifting plants for faecal-free wastewater*, which contains testing requirements.

It should be noted that BS EN 12050-2:2001 does not require the use of macerators (devices that shred any solids in the flow), only that the plant has a solids-handling capacity of 8mm, and this is suitable for normal waste from baths, showers and washbasins.

If the pumping unit also takes flows from a WC or a sink, it should either incorporate a macerator or use larger pumps and pipework and be specified to:

*   BS EN 12050-1:2001 *Wastewater lifting plants for buildings and sites. Principles of construction and testing. Lifting plants for wastewater containing faecal matter*;
*   where the number of users is small and the plant serves no more than a single WC to which it is directly connected, one washbasin, one shower and one bidet located in the same room as the WC to BS EN 12050-3:2001 *Wastewater lifting plants for buildings and sites. Principles of construction and testing. Lifting plants for wastewater containing faecal matter for limited applications.*

The layout and pipework of the lifting plant should be designed in accordance with BS EN 12056-4:2000.

In the event of a failure of a macerator or pump (e.g. due to blockage or failure of controls or power), users must be able to use another sanitary appliance which does not rely on pumping in order to ensure continued access to sanitary accommodation.

> The drainage of baths, showers, bidets and washbasins must comply with the requirements of AD H1.

Baths, showers, bidets and washbasins should be emptied to an adequate system of drainage via:

- a grating (to retain solid matter which could otherwise lead to blockages of the drainage system and increase the loading on sewage treatment plant);
- a trap (to prevent foul gas coming from the drains);
- fixed pipework.

5.6   Relevant British Standards and other guidance

Reference	Publisher	Obtain and read?
Approved Document H – Drainage and waste disposal	CLG	Optional for layout; essential for detailed design
BS EN 12056-1:2000 *Gravity drainage systems inside buildings. Part 1: General and performance requirements*		Optional for layout
BS EN 12056-2:2000 *Gravity drainage systems inside buildings. Part 2: Sanitary pipework, layout and calculation*	BSI	Optional for layout; essential for detailed design
BS EN 12056-4:2000 *Gravity drainage systems inside buildings. Part 4: Wastewater lifting plants – Layout and calculation*	BSI	Optional for layout; essential for detailed design if pumping is used
BS EN 12050-1:2001 *Wastewater lifting plants for buildings and sites. Principles of construction and testing. Lifting plants for wastewater containing faecal matter*	BSI	Optional – but use in specifications of packaged pumping units
BS EN 12050-3:2001 *Wastewater lifting plants for buildings and sites. Principles of construction and testing. Lifting plants for wastewater containing faecal matter for limited applications*	BSI	Optional – but use in specifications of packaged pumping units
BS 6465-1:2006 *Sanitary installations. Code of practice for the design of sanitary facilities and scales of provision of sanitary and associated appliances*	BSI	Essential for buildings other than houses
BS 6465-2:1996 *Sanitary installations. Code of practice for space requirements for sanitary appliances*	BSI	Essential for layout
BS 6465-3:2006 *Sanitary installations. Code of practice for the selection, installation and maintenance of sanitary and associated appliances*	BSI	Optional
Water Fittings and Materials Directory	Water Regulations Advisory Scheme	Essential for checking that fitting and materials comply with the Water Regulations
Water Regulations Guide	WRc	Essential for detailed design and installation of water supply systems

Food preparation areas (G6)

6.1 The requirement

 FOOD PREPARATION AREAS

G6
A suitable sink must be provided in any area where food is prepared

Limits on application
None.

6.2 Sinks

The preparation of food also involves washing of kitchenware and utensils. However, if this is carried out in a separate room using a dishwasher, it is not necessary to provide an additional sink in that room.

A sink is defined as 'a receptacle used for holding water (for preparation of food or washing up) supplied through a tap and having a waste pipe'.

Sinks in food preparation areas must also be supplied with cold and hot wholesome water (requirements G1 and G3 respectively).

The Workplace (Health, Safety and Welfare) Regulations 1992 (for more detail about these regulations, refer to Chapter 4) do not specifically require the provision of sinks. However, they do require that all fixtures and fittings in workplaces should be kept clean, and designed and installed so as to allow them to be effectively cleaned. This statement of good practice is also given in BS 6465-3:2006. BS 6465-1:2006+A1:2009 gives recommendations for the provision of cleaners' sinks in various types of buildings, as well as kitchen sinks.

BS 6465-3:2006 provides detailed advice on selection of sink type, installation and maintenance.

BS 6465-2:1998 gives guidance on the spaces required for the sink itself and for its use (typically 500mm in front of the sink).

The Food Standards Agency's Code of Practice, *Food Hygiene – a Guide for Businesses*, gives advice on complying with the Food Hygiene Regulations[1] in areas where food and drink are prepared. Although the regulations require hygienic conditions in areas where food is handled, they do not provide details of requirements. The code emphasises the need for effective hand washing, and states that washbasins must be used only for washing hands. Although not stated explicitly, recognised practice is that sinks should not be used for hand washing in order to prevent harmful bacteria from spreading from people's hands to food, equipment, etc. The code also advises that, where necessary, there should be a separate sink for washing food. The local environmental health officer should be contacted for requirements.

A sink has a flat bottom to facilitate standing items upright, such as washing-up bowls, pots and pans.

A basin has a rounded bottom, to reduce the volume of water needed to give a depth suitable for washing in.

6.3   Dishwashers

Dishwashers have benefits and disadvantages in terms of water and energy use when compared with washing up in a sink, as shown in Table 18.

Because a sink is used for purposes other than washing up and is required by G6, a dishwasher cannot replace the need for a sink in kitchens. However, the installation of a dishwasher may, depending on the circumstances, enable water savings to be made, provided it is fully loaded and crockery etc. is not rinsed before being put into the dishwasher.

The Water Efficiency Calculator makes an allowance for a dishwasher to be fitted (whether initially or at some time in the future).

6.4   Drainage

The drainage of sinks must comply with the requirements of AD H1.

Sinks should be emptied to an adequate system of drainage by way of:

- a grating (to retain solid matter which could otherwise lead to blockages of the drainage system and increase the loading on sewage treatment plant);
- a trap (to prevent foul gas coming from the drains);
- fixed pipework.

Table 18
Comparison between washing by hand and dishwashers

Feature	Washing by hand in a sink	Dishwasher
Cleansing efficiency	Better for removal of baked-on waste (subject to operator)	Better for washing crockery and utensils – owing to high temperature and use of more aggressive detergents
Space	Space already provided	Additional space needed
Electrical supply needed	No	Yes
Water and drainage		Additional water and drainage will be required if dishwasher is not located sufficiently close to sink or clothes washing machine to share connection
Other uses (e.g. preparation, clothes washing)	Yes	No – crockery and cooking utensils only
Large utensils	Yes	Limited by size of dishwasher
Water efficiency		
Fully loaded	Typically 13 litres*	Typically 13 litres
Partially loaded	Typically 8 litres*	Around 70% of energy as full load (typically 9 litres)
Energy efficiency	Energy required to heat water	Energy required to heat water (generally hotter than washing up by hand) and pumping, control, etc. Typically 1.05kWh per cycle for a AAA-rated model
Health and safety	Normal height, inconvenient for wheelchair users or children	Floor-mounted machines within reach of children Open doors trip hazard

*Washing by hand is usually more frequent.

6.5   Relevant British Standards and other guidance

Reference	Publisher	Obtain and read?
Approved Document H – Drainage and waste disposal	CLG	Optional for layout purposes; essential for detailed drainage design
BS 6465-1:2006 *Sanitary installations. Code of practice for the design of sanitary facilities and scales of provision of sanitary and associated appliances*	BSI	Essential for buildings other than houses
BS 6465-2:1996 *Sanitary installations. Code of practice for space requirements for sanitary appliances*	BSI	Essential for layout
BS 6465-3:2006 *Sanitary installations. Code of practice for the selection, installation and maintenance of sanitary and associated appliances*	BSI	Optional
Water Regulations Guide	WRc	Essential for detailed design and installation of water supply systems

Note

1.   The Food Hygiene (England) Regulations 2006 (SI 2006/14) and The Food Hygiene (Wales) Regulations 2006 (SI 2006/31 (W.5)).

Appendix

Example of use of Water Efficiency Calculator

The values used in this example have been chosen to demonstrate the use of the Water Efficiency Calculator and should not be taken to be typical or preferred values. Manufacturers' data must be used, as the products stated in the calculation must be those installed.

Example

Assume a large four-bedroom house with the water provisions shown overleaf.

Data

Based upon manufacturer's details, data on the selected fittings are as follows:

WCs

1 @ 6 litre single flush (en-suite bathroom)

1 @ 4/2.6 litre dual flush (cloakroom)

1 @ 6/3 litre dual flush (family bathroom)

Taps (basin and bidet)

1 mixer tap @ 5.0 litres/minute (cloakroom basin)

1 mixer tap @ 7.9 litres/minute (en-suite bathroom bidet)

2 pillar taps @ 6.1 litres/minute each (en-suite bathroom basin)

2 pillar taps @ 5.9 litres/minute each (family bathroom basin)

(Note that the bath taps should not be included.)

Baths

1 @ 140 litres capacity to overflow (family bathroom)

1 @ 170 litres capacity to overflow (en-suite bathroom)

Shower

1 @ 12.3 litres/minute (family bathroom)

Sink taps

1 mixer tap @ 11.9 litres/minute (kitchen sink)

2 pillar taps @ 8.9 litres/minute each (utility room sink)

Washing machine

Type not known – to be provided by householder.

Dishwasher

Type not known – to be provided by householder.

Multiple fittings

Use Table 2 from the Water Efficiency Calculator.

Room	Sink	Dishwasher	Washing machine	WC	Basin	Bath	Shower	Bidet	Waste disposal unit	Water softener
Kitchen	1	1								
Utility room	1		1							
Family bathroom				1	1	1	1			
En-suite bathroom				1	1	1		1		
Cloakroom				1	1					

WCs

Table 19a
Consumption calculator for multiple fittings for new dwellings (WCs) (Table 2.7)

WC type	Effective flushing volume* (litres) (a)	Quantity (no.) (b)	Total per fitting type (c) = (a) × (b)
1 (6 litres)	6	1	6.00
2 (4/2.6 litres)	(4 × 0.33) + (2.6 x 0.67) = 3.06	1	3.06
3 (6/3 litres)	(6 × 0.33) + (3 × 0.67) = 3.99	1	3.99
4			
Total (Sum of all quantities) (d)		3	
Total (Sum of all totals per fitting type) (e)			13.05
Average effective flushing volume (litres) (e/d)			4.35

*The effective flushing volume for dual-flush WCs is calculated as [full-flushing volume (litres) × 0.33] = [part-flushing volume (litres) x 0.67].

As there are multiple WCs, enter '0' for the WC (single flush) and WC (double flush) and enter '4.35' for WC (multiple fittings) into Table 1 of the Water Efficiency Calculator.

Taps

Table 19b
Consumption calculator for multiple fittings for new dwellings (taps) (Table 2.3)

Tap fitting type	Flow rate (l/min) (a)	Quantity (no.) (b)	Total per fitting type (c) = (a) × (b)
1 (mixer)	5.0	1	5.0
2 (mixer)	7.9	1	7.9
3 (pillar)	6.1	2	12.2
4 (pillar)	5.9	2	11.8
Total (Sum of all quantities) (d)		6	
Total (Sum of all totals per fitting type) (e)			36.9
Highest flow rate (l/min) (e/d)			6.15
Proportionate flow rate (l/min) (f)			7.9
Weighted average flow rate (l/min) (f) × 0.7			5.53

As the average flow rate is greater than the proportionate flow rate, enter the value '6.15' under 'Taps' in Table 1 of the Water Efficiency Calculator.

Baths

Table 19c
Consumption calculator for multiple fittings for new dwellings (baths) (Table 2.2)

Bath fitting type	Capacity to overflow (litres) (a)	Quantity (b)	Total per fitting type (c) = (a) × (b)
1	140	1	140
2	170	1	170
3			
4			
Total (Sum of all quantities) (d)		2	
Total (Sum of all totals per fitting type) (e)			310
Average capacity to overflow (e/d)			155
Highest capacity to overflow (litres) (f)			170
Proportionate average capacity to overflow (litres) (f) × 0.7			119

As the average capacity is greater than the proportionate capacity, enter the value '155' under 'Baths (where shower also present)' in Table 1 of the Water Efficiency Calculator.

Enter the value '0' under 'Bath only' to avoid double-counting.

Kitchen/utility taps

Table 19d
Consumption calculator for multiple fittings for new dwellings (kitchen/utility taps) (Table 2.3)

Tap fitting type	Flow rate (l/min) (a)	Quantity (no.) (b)	Total per fitting type (c) = (a) × (b)
1 (mixer)	11.9	1	11.9
2 (pillar)	8.9	2	17.8
3			
4			
Total (Sum of all quantities)	(d)	3	
Total (Sum of all quantities)		(e)	29.7
Average flow rate (l/min)		(e/d)	9.90
Highest flow rate (l/min)		(f)	11.9
Proportionate flow rate (l/min)		(f) × 0.7	8.33

As the average flow rate is higher than the proportionate flow rate, insert '9.90' into Table 1 of the Water Efficiency Calculator.

Other fittings

Washing machine

Enter '8.17' in Table 1 of the Water Efficiency Calculator as the default value.

Dishwasher

Enter '1.25' in Table 1 of the Water Efficiency Calculator as the default value.

Water softener

Enter '0' in Table 1 of the Water Efficiency Calculator as none fitted.

Sink waste disposal unit

Enter '0' in Table 1 of the Water Efficiency Calculator as none fitted.

Table 1

The first page of Table 1 of the Water Efficiency Calculator can now be filled in, giving the daily volume of water used inside the building per person.

Table 20
The Water Efficiency Calculator for New Dwellings (Table 1)

Installation type	Unit of measure	Capacity/ flow rate	Use factor	Fixed use (litres/ person/ day)	Litres/ person/day = (1 × 2) + 3
		(1)	(2)	(3)	(4)
WC (single flush)	Flush volume (litres)	0	4.42	0.00	0
WC (dual flush)	Full-flush volume (litres)	0	1.46	0.00	0
	Part-flush volume (litres)	0	2.96	0.00	0
WC (multiple fittings)	Average effective flushing volume (litres)	4.35	4.42	0.00	19.23
Taps (excluding kitchen taps)	Flow rate (l/min)	6.15	1.58	1.58	11.30
Bath (where shower also present)	Capacity to overflow (litres)	155	0.11	0.00	17.05
Shower (where bath also present)	Flow rate (l/min)	12.3	4.37	0.00	53.75
Bath only	Capacity to overflow (litres)	0	0.50	0.00	0
Shower only	Flow rate (l/min)	0	5.60	0.00	0
Kitchen utility room sink taps	Flow rate (l/min)	9.9	0.44	10.36	14.72
Washing machine	Litres per kg dry load	8.17	2.1	0.00	17.16
Dishwasher	Litres per place setting	1.25	3.6	0.00	4.50
Waste disposal unit	Litres per use	If present = 1 If absent = 0	3.08	0.00	0
Water softener	Litres/day		1.00	0.00	0
	(5)	Total calculated use (litres/person/ day) = column 4			137.71

Rainwater harvesting – Table 5

To minimise the use of wholesome water, rainwater harvesting will be installed for toilet flushing.

The area of roof to be drained is 144m² and the average annual rainfall is 850mm. The yield coefficient and filter efficiency is 0.69.

The number of people in the house is calculated as:

Master bedroom	2
Other bedrooms	3
Calculated occupancy	5

Calculated volume of rainfall availability per person, using Table 5.1 of the Water Efficiency Calculator.

Table 21
Rainwater collection calculation for new dwellings – BS 8515 *Intermediate approach* (Table 5.1)

Collection area (m²)	(a)	144
Yield coefficient and hydraulic filter efficiency, e.g. 0.7	(b)	0.69
Rainfall average (mm/year)	(c)	850
Daily rainwater collection (litres)	[(a) × (b) × (c)]/365 = (a)	231.4
Number of occupants	(e)	5
Daily rainwater per person (litres)	(d)/(e) = (f)	46.28

Table 22
Rainwater saving calculations for new dwellings (Table 5.5)

		Litres/person/day
Rainwater collected	(a)	46.28
Rainwater demand	(b)	19.23
Rainwater savings	(c) = (a)/(b)* (b)	19.23

Daily volume used for WC flushing (from Table 1) is 19.23 litres per person. As there is more rainwater available per person than is used for WC flushing, enter '19.23' in Table 1 of the Water Efficiency Calculator.

The second part of Table 1 of the Water Efficiency Calculator can now be completed.

Table 23
The Water Efficiency Calculator for New Dwellings (Table 1)

Installation type	Unit of measure	Capacity/flow rate	Use factor	Fixed use (litres/person/day)	Litres/person/day = (1 × 2) + 3
		(1)	(2)	(3)	(4)
	(6)	Contribution from greywater (litres/person/day) from Table 4.6			0
	(7)	Contribution from rainwater (litres/person/day) from Table 5.5			19.23
	(8)	Normalisation factor			0.91
	(9)	Total water consumption (*Code for Sustainable Homes*) = (5 – 6 – 7) × 8 (litres/person/day)			107.82
	(10)	External water use			5.0
	(11)	Total water consumption (Part G) = 9 +1 (litres/person/day)			112.8

Therefore the calculated wholesome water consumption is 112.8 litres per person per day, which is less than the maximum permitted value of 125 litres per person per day.

Glossary

Approved inspector	A company or an individual authorised under the Building Act 1984 to carry out inspections to help achieve compliance with the Building Regulations in England and Wales. A list of approved inspectors can be viewed at the Association of Consultant Approved Inspectors (ACAI) website (www.acai.org.uk).
Building control body (BCB)	An approved inspector or local authority building control service, responsible for helping to achieve compliance with the Building Regulations.
Building notice	A means of applying for Building Regulations approval from the local authority building control service. Plans are not required and work is inspected on site. It is quicker than submitting plans for approval but there is a risk of having to correct any non-compliant work. They cannot be used for building work which is subject to section 1 of the Fire Precautions Act 1971 or Part II of the Fire Precautions (Workplace) Regulations 1997; for work which will be built close to or over the top of rain water and foul drains shown on the 'map of sewers'; and where a new building will front onto a private street. They are valid for three years. A local authority is not required to issue a completion certificate.
Building Regulations Advisory Committee (BRAC)	Advisory body to government regarding building regulation matters.
Chartered Institute of Building Services Engineers (CIBSE)	A professional body that exists to provide standards, information and education about building services. It also speaks for the profession on matters relating to construction, engineering and sustainability.
Communities and Local Government (CLG)	The government department responsible for, amongst other things, the Building Regulations in England and Wales.
Competent person self-certification scheme	A scheme that enables people who have been assessed as competent to certify that the work they have undertaken complies with the Building Regulations.
Completion certificate	A statement issued by the BCB (following a satisfactory completion inspection of the completed works) that certifies that the work complies with the Building Regulations.
Controlled service	A service on which the Building Regulations imposes a requirement. These are listed in Schedule 1 of the Building Regulations 2000 (as amended).

Code for Sustainable Homes (CSH)	Government document intended to make new homes in the UK more sustainable, including their use of water.
Department for Environment, Food and Rural Affairs (Defra)	UK government department responsible for, amongst other things, water resources.
Diameter nominal (DN)	Nominal size of a pipe, a convenient round number approximately equal to either its internal or external diameter.
Greywater	Wastewater not containing faecal matter or urine. After suitable treatment, greywater can be used for toilet flushing, irrigation or clothes washing and therefore normally includes discharges from baths, washbasins and showers but excludes WCs, urinals, bidets and sinks.
Historic building	Includes listed buildings (i.e. buildings included on the statutory List of Buildings of Special Architectural or Historic Interest); buildings situated in conservation areas; buildings which are of architectural or historical interest; buildings within National Parks, Areas of Outstanding Natural Beauty and World Heritage Sites; and buildings in historic parks and gardens or in the curtilages of Scheduled Ancient Monuments.
Home Information Pack (HIP)	A set of documents, supplied by a house vendor, giving potential purchasers information about that property, such as energy usage and now water efficiency. Required for most homes put on the market for sale with vacant possession in England and Wales.
Notice of completion of commissioning	Notice given by the person who has commissioned the installation (i.e. adjusted and tested it to achieve the specified performance) that the commissioning has been satisfactorily carried out to an approved procedure.
Regulation 17K	Regulation 17K under the Building Regulations 2000 (as amended) which requires that for any new dwelling the potential wholesome water consumption of its occupants should not exceed 125 litres per person per day when calculated using the Water Efficiency Calculator for New Dwellings.
Sanitary facilities	Toilets and places to wash and bathe.
Softened wholesome water	Water that would be wholesome, except that its sodium content exceeds 20mg/Na/litre because of softening.
Tundish	Funnel that forms part of a pipeline, where the discharge flows through air to prevent backflow and to allow flows to be seen.
Thermostatic mixing valve (TMV)	Device for automatically introducing cold water into the hot water system close to the outlet, to limit the delivered temperature of hot water.

Unvented hot water storage systems (UHWSS)	Hot water storage system at mains pressure.
Vented system	Hot water storage system that is at atmospheric pressure (i.e. it has an open vent to air).
Water efficiency	Using no more water than necessary.
Wholesome water	Water that is fit for drinking, cooking, food preparation or washing without any potential danger to human health by meeting stringent requirements laid down in regulations.
Water Regulations Advisory Service (WRAS)	Body set up to test and certify products and materials for compliance with the Water Regulations.

Index